Project Myopia

Allan Kelly

Project Myopia

Allan Kelly

ISBN 978-1-912832-04-0

Leanpub

This is a Leanpub book. Leanpub empowers authors and publishers with the Lean Publishing process. Lean Publishing is the act of publishing an in-progress ebook using lightweight tools and many iterations to get reader feedback, pivot until you have the right book and build traction once you do.

© 2015 - 2018 Allan Kelly

Contents

Free Book i

Project Myopia iii

Prologue v

1. **Introduction** 1
2. **Agile project tension** 5
3. **Project problems** 11
   3.1 Why critique? 12
   3.2 Projects exist 13
4. **Defining a project** 15
   4.1 Developers' definition 16
   4.2 Dictionary definition 18
   4.3 PMI definition 19
   4.4 PRINCE2 definition 22
   4.5 The defining feature 23
   4.6 Counter-argument 24
   4.7 Definitions of success 27
   4.8 In conclusion 28

CONTENTS

5. **Diseconomies of scale** 31
   - 5.1 Milk is cheaper in large cartons 32
   - 5.2 Evidence of diseconomies 35
   - 5.3 Think diseconomies, think small 40
   - 5.4 Economies of scale thinking prevails 41
   - 5.5 And projects... 42
   - 5.6 Making small decisions 43
   - 5.7 Optimize for small 44
   - 5.8 Kelly's Laws 45

6. **Software isn't temporary** 47

7. **If they use it, it will change** 53
   - 7.1 Counter-argument 56
   - 7.2 Conclusion 59

8. **False projects** 61

9. **The problem with project success** 63
   - 9.1 Project assumptions 64
   - 9.2 Goal displacement 65

10. **Multiple projects** 69
    - 10.1 A model 69
    - 10.2 Project A 70
    - 10.3 Project B 72
    - 10.4 Interleave A and B 73
    - 10.5 Split the team 74
    - 10.6 Enter Project C 75
    - 10.7 What does this illustrate? 76
    - 10.8 Assumptions 77

11.	Increasing value		81
	11.1	Value-seeking	83
	11.2	Reducing risk	86

12.	Debt thinking		89
	12.1	Debt is good	90
	12.2	Why pay back debt?	91
	12.3	Payday loans	92
	12.4	Technical liabilities	93

13.	The quality problem		95
	13.1	Rethinking the quality tradeoff	98
	13.2	The cost of poor quality	99
	13.3	Who pays?	101
	13.4	External costs	102
	13.5	There's no such thing as quick and dirty	103

14.	Programmes not projects		105
	14.1	What does a Programme Manager do?	106
	14.2	The Programme Management Office	106
	14.3	So what is a programme?	108

15.	Personal changes		109
	15.1	Stop saying "project"	110
	15.2	Collections of small things	110
	15.3	Public success criteria	110
	15.4	Value estimates	111
	15.5	More than agile	111
	15.6	Stronger together	112
	15.7	Continuous Digital	113

Continuous Digital 115

CONTENTS

Evolution of a meme 117

About the author 119
    Also by Allan Kelly 120

Acknowledgements 123

Free Book

Xanpan is available for free

Xanpan: Team Centric Agile Software Development is available for free to all subscribers to Allan Kelly's newsletter[1]

---

[1] https://www.allankellyassociates.co.uk/xanpan_offer/

Project Myopia

Project Myopia: The belief that the project model is the only way of managing business change and development. Not seeing digital development as a continuing commitment to growing the business, but instead believing it will end and working towards that end.

Type 1 Project Myopia: Success

Failing to recognize that meeting project success criteria is not the same as successfully delivering business benefit. Project success criteria may actually reduce business benefit in the short term, and even more in the long term.

Type 2 Project Myopia: Beyond the project

Failure to see that successful change, transformation, services and products have a long life after the end of a project. Products and services need to continue changing if they are to succeed. Ongoing change, enhancements and renewal need to be a way of life.

Type 3 Project Myopia: Digital Business

Failure to understand that for digital business to survive and grow, digital technology needs to advance in tandem with the business. Halting digital progress halts business progress.

Business change and transformation, product development and maintenance don't need to be set up as a project.

Prologue

Practical men, who believe themselves to be quite exempt from any intellectual influence, are usually the slaves of some defunct economist. John Maynard Keynes, economist, 1883-1946

When I attended the Lean Agile Scotland conference to deliver the #NoProjects presentation I met a group of people from an Edinburgh financial services company. This group could not comprehend work without projects. Yet when I quizzed them I discovered that the same people had worked on the same software code base, on the same mainframe, to serve the same customers for over a decade. One project followed another; the only thing that was temporary about their work was the end dates.

The financial services company did not consider itself a digital company, let alone a software company, but its very ability to do business depended on information technology and software. Take away the software or finish the software and the company could not operate. It was a digital company whether it knew it or not.

At times technology management, indeed perhaps all modern management, seems to revolve around 'projects' as if they are an inherently natural phenomenon: they are not. Projects are a twentieth-century invention that has outlived its usefulness.

The project model sidelines business benefit because it chases the wrong goals in the wrong way. Traditional project planning is not a harmless, benign, past time. It is dangerous, it reduces value and increases risk.

The project model does not describe the world of software development or the digital business world. Forcing software development into the project model requires so much mental energy, compromise, and workarounds that it becomes impossible to see what is really happening.

Managers and engineers who cling to the project model to describe their work are like aircraft ground crew that use manuals for a Supermarine Spitfire to service a Lockheed F-35 Lightning. Both are agile single-seat fighters with wings, but that is where the similarity ends.

Nowhere is this mismatch more apparent than in teams who practice continuous delivery. Such teams will inevitably abandon the project model, a model made for a temporary world.

Continuous is not temporary.

1. Introduction

> *Basic to successful project management is recognizing when the project is needed – in other words, when to form a project, as opposed to when to use the regular functional organization to do the job.*
> Cleland and King[1], Systems Analysis and Project Management, 1968

The simple fact is that there are projects and there is other stuff. All work does not have to be a project. However, it sometimes seems that many organizations have forgotten this fact. Projects are not the only way to organize work. Project management is not the only way to manage work.

There is work that fits the project model and can – even should – get managed as 'a project'. Then there is work that does not fit the model. Managing such work as 'a project' can hinder the work and be harmful to the final product. Software development is an example of the latter. Managing software development work using the project model makes the work more difficult than it needs to be. The project model can reduce the value of the product and result in an inferior product.

There are those who tell me that in rejecting the project model I 'fail to see the bigger picture'. In return I would say that the

---
[1] *Systems Analysis and Project Management*, David I. Cleland and William R. King, 1968. Excerpt taken from https://en.wikiquote.org/wiki/Project_management

opposite is true. It is because I see the bigger picture that I reject the project model. Certainly to view software development as coding alone is to ignore the 'bigger picture'. Yet to view all software development as a project – especially a defined project – is to ignore an even bigger picture.

There have long been problems in applying project management to software development. Look at the failure rate of software projects, and contrast that failure rate with the omnipresence of software-powered technology in our modern lives. Software development has succeeded *despite* the application of the project model, not because of it.

These problems have become more acute and pressing because of two forces. The first of these is the rise of agile development.

Agile software development has made the problems with the project model more apparent. As is so often the case, agile highlights existing problems and challenges workers to fix them. When agile teams are successful the limitations of the project model are even clearer. Success creates tension between agile teams and those who commission the teams.

The tensions between agile working and the project model are visible to anyone who must manage or govern projects. Successful agile teams working under the project model need to satisfy two conflicting regimes.

The arrival of *Continuous Delivery*[2] (CD) and *DevOps* added further tension. These approaches challenge the assumption of temporary built into the project model. Projects can be surprisingly long-lived, but the model used to manage them rests on the

---

[2] *Continuous Delivery: Reliable Software Releases through Build, Test, and Deployment Automation*, Humble and Farley, 2010.

assumption of temporary. Continuous is not temporary. CD was always embedded inside agile, but as people unlearn the project model and technology advances, CD becomes a potent force.

Reconciling the project model with agile development and CD has become more difficult, and the mismatch more obvious to practitioners. The project model itself has become an impediment to advancement.

While the incompatibility of agile working and CD with the project model makes life hard, it is a second and more important force that is challenging project thinking: the rise of *Digital Business*.

At its most crude, digital business is business based on software technology. For digital businesses to continue, to grow and to be competitive they must continue to improve the software that underpins them.

When a business is a digital business the routine work – the work the business does every day – is digital work, and digital work implies software. Improving the business means improving the software that powers the work. So improving software is itself routine work, work the business exists to do and work the business needs to be organized to do.

Businesses that end are usually seen as failures. Yet the project model regards reaching the *end* as a success in its own right. The rise of digital business makes it critical for companies to find a new model for managing and governing their technology work.

In this book I outline the problems involved in applying the project model to software development and digital business. While I make a few suggestions for how to improve things, this book is a critique. The companion book, *Continuous Digital*[3] sets out the alternative, continuous model.

[3] https://leanpub.com/cdigital/

2. Agile project tension

To claim that projects are not undertaken in agile environments would be wrong. Agile teams undertake 'projects' all the time. Indeed, there is a large collection of literature and training that specifically discusses project management in an agile context – it's even possible to get certification in Agile Project Management.

If one examines the goals and aims of project management they can be surprisingly similar to the aims and goals behind agile. But from a common starting position the two schools develop radically different management models. Applying the project model and the agile model at the same time to the same software effort invariably creates tensions. The fundamental assumptions underlying the two models are different even if the goals are the same.

As a result proactive Project Managers and Scrum Masters devote much of their time to managing these tensions. Indeed, some executives even claim that using two models deliberately creates tension in order to control work. Yet software development and digital business are hard enough without deliberately adding complications and easy scapegoats for when things go wrong. Since the project model and the agile model have different, almost contradictory, definitions of success and failure, at some point *failure* will occur.

Many if not most teams faced with working with agile in a project model never manage or resolve these tensions: instead they just ignore them. There are plenty of coders and testers who would not recognize the PMI or PRINCE2 definition of a project. Equally, there are plenty of Project Managers who view agile as a series of mini-projects.

Such views may well work on a day-to-day basis and serve to lessen an individual's cognitive dissonance, but they neither promote effective working nor make for good governance. Sooner or later one view comes to dominate: either the project model asserts itself and neuters agile working, or agile working renders the project model redundant. The 'projects' these teams work on are little more than accounting conventions and are a long way removed from the PMI and PRINCE2 models.

Some of the more obvious tensions between the project model and the agile model include:

- The agile model sees each small piece of work (for example a story) as a potential deliverable, while the project model aims to deliver a whole.
- The agile model optimizes for small, while the project model optimizes for large.
- In prioritizing work by business value the agile model inherently accepts that some work will fall off the end. Conversely, in the project model anything less than everything is failure.
- The agile model embraces changing requirements and specifications, while the project model aims to 'control' or even eliminate such changes ('scope creep').
- The project model expects teams to be temporary organizations, while the agile model values stable long-lived teams.

- The project model sees 'quality' as a variable one can dial up and down, while the agile model sees consistently high quality as a prerequisite for effective working and delivery.
- The project model assumes that a small number of individuals can initially scope, plan, define and design work. Then a larger group of individuals can implement the plan – *a simple matter of programming*. The agile model seeks to engage all workers in meaningful decisions about scope, plans, work definitions and design.

This list could go on. Each point of tension can be managed, but such tensions obscure what is happening and increase the mental load on workers. At some point one needs to ask "Is this model fit for purpose?"

Where the two models coexist, individuals need to engage in mental gymnastics – *double-think* – to reconcile the contradictory assumptions. In extreme cases such tensions are enough to destroy the work effort, but more commonly tension simply increases costs and risk while reducing the benefit delivered.

Sometimes tension only becomes apparent when looking across projects. For example, if an agile team is prioritizing work by business value, then one can expect a point to come at which all the high-value work is complete and the team is working on low-value requests. One might also expect their next project to contain some high-value items. The agile mind asks:

> "Why should a team undertake the low-value work to finish the first project when moving directly to the high-value work of the next project will produce a higher return?"

Even if all the work in both projects is completed one day, a cost-of-delay analysis would show that bringing forward high-value items and postponing low-value items would increase the total value delivered. On the other hand, one might ask:

> "Who really cares about the low-value tail end of a project after all?"

Fundamentally the project model defines and constrains work in order to control it, while the agile model embraces emergent needs and changing constraints. The project model is itself an attempt to constrain agility.

For non-software businesses – banks, airlines, high street retailers and so on – such tension can just about be managed. The tension might be troubling and sap energy for the workers who toil day-in, day-out inside organizations at the code-face, but away from the code-face in the executive suite things carry on much the same: project, project, project...

But not for much longer?

When the business is digital the business is a software business. *Finished* is by definition a failure.

Workers can choose who they work for, and the best are no longer choosing to work in such environments. If a company wants the best workers it can't ask them to practice double-think.

The costs of running two models, the agile model and the project model, is too high for digital businesses. The obvious costs are high already – the Project Manager and the Scrum Master, the Gantt charts and the burn-down charts – but the hidden costs are much higher:

- 'Successful' projects that fail to deliver business value.
- The reduced reactivity – *agility* – imposed by the need to shoehorn all work into a project model: to write a requirements document, design an architecture and assemble yet another temporary team.
- The lost knowledge and capability that occurs when a successful team completes the project and is disbanded. Or the hurdles and barriers managers need to jump through to keep teams together, to keep knowledge in the building.
- The loss of clarity and understanding as individuals translate from project-speak to agile-speak and back again.

Not to mention projects that fail despite all the good agile tools that get used.

A digital business can only succeed as a digital business if it is an agile business. It is no use claiming to be a digital business if it takes 27 months to introduce a new feature to match a competitor's product.

It is no longer enough for digital businesses to be 'agile in the engine room', or practice 'agile project delivery'. A digital business needs to be digital and agile all the way through.

Digital businesses that fail to utilize agile strategy and tactics will, sooner or later, meet a competitor that does. Applying yesterday's management models to tomorrow's technology only goes so far.

3. Project problems

The project model has multiple problems: it is a poor guide for managing software development work. The hashtag #NoProjects began life as a discussion of these problems. The following chapters discuss why the project model is a bad fit for software development, why it increases costs and why it destroys value.

Some offer the product model as an alternative to the project model. While the product model is a better match for software development, the two models are not symmetrical alternatives. Rather they address different issues even though they overlap. As such Project Myopia and #NoProject go beyond simply arguing that project management can complement product management.

Key to the #NoProjects critique is the observation that the development of commercially successful software is never finished. Unsuccessful software certainly finishes. When software is successful the use of the software creates the need – and opportunities – for change. Not enhancing the software hinders its usefulness. Prematurely curtailing change also curtails benefits. Therefore all successful software is a product and needs to be managed as a long-lasting product. Using the project model to deliver a series of product increments (as many development organizations do) is short-sighted and hinders value creation.

Fundamentally the project model is about temporary while successful products have longevity. This mismatch imposes costs: management overhead, technical liabilities and, most of all, lost value. In the past companies could get away with this, but in the digital age short-sighted project thinking exacts too high a price.

3.1 Why critique?

Why write a book critiquing the project model? There are really two reasons.

Firstly, many businesses already have a pretty good way of working even with the project model. Such businesses can take a shortcut: just stop talking about projects, ban the word, and carry on working as you were but without all the project rigmarole.

There are some tell-tale signs that a business falls into this category:

- Project B follows Project A, after which comes Project C. Each project deals with the same platform/service/codebase and employs most of the same people.
- Projects start at the start of a new financial year and finish at the end of a financial year.
- You have work-steams, platforms and themes to guide your work as well as projects.

Such companies can simply start by banning the word 'project' and adopting new vocabulary.

In my capacity as an agile consultant, I get asked:

"What is the hardest part of agile?"

I answer:

> "The hard bit is not what you have to learn, it's what you have to unlearn; the things you have to stop doing and the processes you need to take away."

Simply unlearning the project model is a great starting point.

The second reason for looking in detail at the failings of the project model is to learn from it. Some things within the model are good and deserve retention (deadlines, for example), but much else causes problems (temporary teams, for example.) These are things that a new model should avoid.

3.2 Projects exist

I'm not stupid: software projects do exist. I see software projects all the time. I've worked on software projects throughout my career: as a programmer, as a manager and as a consultant. I've even held the title of 'Project Manager' on occasions.

Nor do I deny that you will meet external customers and internal colleagues who want you to 'do a project'. I won't even deny that 'the customer is always right', and if the customer is offering good money for you to do a software project then your company might be stupid for turning the work down.

Most of all I am not saying the project model is everywhere and always flawed. It might be: I don't know. My expertise is in software development, the underpinning of the digital business revolution. I confine my argument to this domain; I'm happy to speculate about extending the argument, but right now I make few claims beyond digital business and software development.

What I am saying is: the project model contains flaws when used for managing the development of software systems, especially software systems on which businesses depend. While the model can be – indeed has been – used for exactly this purpose, the flaws in the model in this context mean reduced value and magnified management problems.

When customers ask you to undertake a project you might want to consider educating them in the alternatives. Part of this education might be to highlight the difficulties of the project model.

In the short term your company may still need to undertake software projects. In the long term, your company stands to make more money and create happier customers by following an alternative model.

As the digital revolution advances, the long term gets closer.

4. Defining a project

> *The problems are dissolved in the actual sense of the word – like a lump of sugar in water.* Ludwig Wittgenstein, philosopher, 1889-1951

What is a project?

It might seem a silly question, but it is an important one. It might also seem that I'm playing word games, but the meaning of words is important.

In October 2014 I delivered 'Beyond Projects' at the Agile Tour conference in London: back then the *no projects hypothesis* was relatively new. A couple of hours later over drinks a programmer approached me to say: "The definition of project you showed... I've never thought that of a project that way."

In fact I'd shown *two* definitions of project, one from the American Project Management Institute and one from the British PRINCE2 standard.

Think about this for a moment. This programmer was working in a project environment, but his understanding of the approach to management, the project management model, was different than the one his managers, specifically his project manager, was using. As a result his goals and aims were different than those of his mangers'.

Again and again I find that programmers (and testers too) think a *software project* is almost a synonym for *software application*:

that it, is a description of some source files and the build scripts, or simply a management term for describing the collection of people and resources building a software system. But to their managers, and especially project managers, the term 'project' mean something different.

It is as if two teams are playing football. One team is playing Association Rules Football (aka *Soccer*), while the other team is playing Rugby Union Football. Worse still, the coaches and managers on the sidelines believe they are playing American Football. Everyone uses the same word 'football': the common aim of all is to score goals by putting a ball between posts. But that is where the similarities end: the tactics and rules of each are quite different.

So let's talk about what a project actually is...

4.1 Developers' definition

Take a look at this screen shot, taken from the Eclipse IDE documentation[1]:

---

[1] http://armstrap-documentation.readthedocs.org/en/latest/getting-started-eclipse-development-tools.html

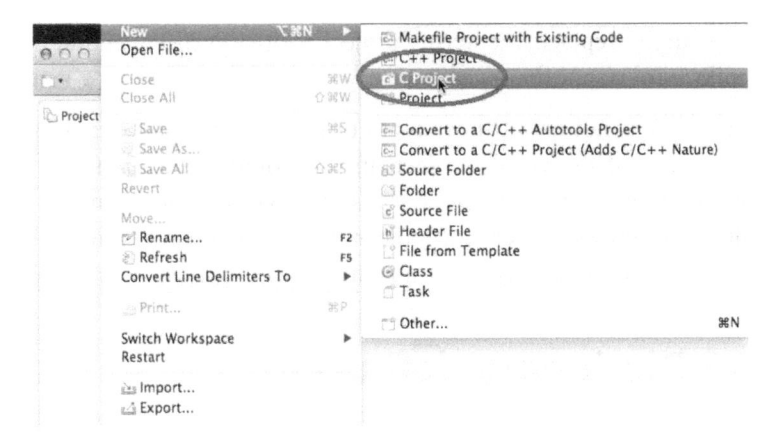

File, New, Project

Or take at look at this definition from Google:

> 'In the Google Developers Console, a project is a collection of settings, credentials, and metadata about the application or applications you're working on that make use of Google Developer APIs and Google Cloud resources'. Google App Engine Console documentation[2]

I don't wish to pick on Eclipse or Google: I could just as easily have talked about Microsoft, IBM, Oracle or Apple products, but one example will suffice. Both these examples, and countless others, illustrate the way programmers typically think about *a project*.

To a programmer a project is a collection of artifacts that go together to help make up a program or executable system.

---

[2] https://developers.google.com/console/help/new/#managingprojects

One might replace the term 'project' with 'parcel', 'bundle', 'collection' or another synonym.

This book is not about these types of project, but the extensive of the use of the word 'project' in this context contributes to the problems with projects. Because the word 'project' means different things to different people in different contexts, common language can hide significant misunderstandings.

4.2 Dictionary definition

The dictionary on my Apple Macintosh offers this definition of the word *project*:

> An individual or collaborative enterprise that is carefully planned to achieve a particular aim: a research project | a project to build a new power station

Turning to my trusty Collins Paperback English Dictionary, and again ignoring the (eight) verbal definitions of 'project', I find these two definitions:

1. a proposal or plan.
2. a detailed study of a particular subject.

These definitions start to point us in the right direction. Projects are somehow entwined with the idea of planning; specifically proposed plans of action. Projects create expectations of detail. There is a belief that projects are planned and are detailed.

That plans are good is frequently taken as self-evident. Newspapers and television news are quick to report that some failure was the 'result of poor planning'. Some managers are fond of saying "Failure to plan is planning to fail". But how many people set out a plan to find their ideal spouse? You may have planned your wedding, but did you also plan the dates and schedules for children? How many readers have a detailed career plan stating who your future employers are?

In truth, many of the most significant events in our lives happen without much planning or analysis.

4.3 PMI definition

The Project Management Institute, founded in 1969, exists to further the practice, and knowledge about, project management. The PMI website says this about *project*[3]:

> What is a project? It's a temporary endeavor undertaken to create a unique product, service or result.
>
> A project is temporary in that it has a defined beginning and end in time, and therefore defined scope and resources.
>
> A project is unique in that it is not a routine operation, but a specific set of operations designed to accomplish a singular goal. So a project team often includes people who don't usually work together –

---

[3] http://www.pmi.org/en/About-Us/About-Us-What-is-Project-Management.aspx

sometimes from different organizations and across multiple geographies.

The development of software for an improved business process, the construction of a building or bridge, the relief effort after a natural disaster, the expansion of sales into a new geographic market – all are projects.

And all must be expertly managed to deliver the on-time, on-budget results, learning and integration that organizations need.

Undoubtedly software development aims to create a unique artifact. In software one can make identical copies of an existing artifact at almost zero cost in almost zero time: select, Control-C, Control-V. The cost of measuring this manufacturing process is usually greater than the cost of manufacturing itself.

However other parts of this definition create problems:

> *A project is unique in that it is not a routine operation... and ...a project team often includes people who don't usually work together...*

For a digital business creating and changing software is a routine event. While much that happens in software development is not routine, the act of doing software development *is* routine. When a team works together day-in day-out for years, writing and testing software every day, a certain routine does develop.

> ...must be expertly managed to deliver the on-time, on-budget results, learning and integration...

As I will argue in the coming chapters, these 'success' criteria (specifically time and budget) lead us astray. But it is the first part of this definition that creates the biggest problems:

> A project is temporary in that it has a defined beginning and end in time, and therefore defined scope and resources.

Traditionally software development teams did try and define 'scope', but this was always difficult and regularly compromised. Teams practicing agile software development frequently forego scope control altogether. Further, as I will argue in the chapters to come, controlling scope not only leads to the loss of business value, but potentially destroys software and companies.

Defined time also creates problems: again, agile teams work with time in a different way than traditional teams. Actually defining when a software project begins can be hard:

> 'The initial difficulty with schedule measurement is a basic one: identifying the starting point of any given project! Very seldom are projects started so crisply and precisely that a manager or user can assert "Project XYZ began on April 25, 2008". [4]

Jones also discusses the difficulty of determining the end date for a software project. While software 'projects' frequently close as

---
[4] *Applied Software Measurement*, Capers Jones, 2008

a 'project', work on the software does not. It may continue as a subsequent project, it may get rolled into another project, it may continue as 'business as usual', or hidden under something else.

Formal project start and end dates in software are at best artificial constructs. Dates might are frequently imposed as part of a management process, but these dates do not correspond to any meaningful events in the software development process.

Still, even given these flaws, the PMI definition is probably the best definition there is.

4.4 PRINCE2 definition

In the UK the PRINCE2 qualification is more popular than the PMI project management qualification: I myself hold one of these certificates. In PRINCE2 a project is:

> 'A temporary organization that is needed to produce a unique and predefined outcome or result at a pre-specified time using predetermined resources'.

This definition shows the same flaws as the PMI definition. Conveniently, my 2005 PRINCE2 manual elaborates on this definition[5]:

> 'A PRINCE2 project, therefore, has the following characteristics:

---
[5] *Managing Successful Projects with PRINCE2*, Office of Government Communication, 2005.

- A finite and defined lifecycle

- Defined and measurable business products

- A corresponding set of activities to achieve the business products

- A defined amount of resources

- An organizational structure, with defined responsibilities, to manage the project'.

Some digital software development efforts might exhibit these characteristics, but on the whole teams tasked with innovation, with creating a platform or service that will be used for years, cannot meet these criteria. The further one moves away from these characteristics, the less the project model – or at least the PRINCE2 method – applies.

4.5 The defining feature

All the formal definitions of 'project' looked at here share one key characteristic: temporary. For the project management industry projects are *temporary* endeavors. Let me suggest that the defining feature of a project, when used by managers to discuss an endeavor, is that:

> *Projects have end dates and come to a close*

4.6 Counter-argument

There are plenty of project aficionados who, if they have read this far, will object to the points I have made so far. They will correctly argue that:

- *Project managers do allow requirements to change; they do not stick doggedly to the initial requests.* This is true, although not universal: there are plenty of project managers who accept that requirements change during the project.
- *Project managers do not needlessly disband teams: they will fight to keep teams together.* Again they are right, although again not universally so. Many project managers recognize that teams do projects, often on the same code base or product, and there is a similar project right behind the current one.
- *Project managers are not stupid about value; they will seek out value and will sacrifice schedule, features and fight for resources if they think they can improve value.* Yet again they are right – although again this stance is not universal.

In fact, plenty of enlightened project managers will find a way of doing the right thing no matter what project doctrine says they should do. But now there is another problem:

> If project managers don't follow the project doctrine, then what do they follow? What do they manage? And how do they manage?
>
> If projects don't doggedly stick to PMI and PRINCE2 type definitions of what 'a project is', then what

exactly is a project? And why are these people called 'project managers'?

And if none of these conditions holds true, then why are project managers trained in these definitions and approaches? What is the profession based on?

These definitions underly project manager training from PMI and PRINCE2, but the definitions are, at least for software development, flawed, so by implication training (and certification) derived from these definitions also contains flaws. In environments where these definitions are valid, such training has validity. When these definitions do not describe the domain, then the definitions, plus the training and processes built on such understanding, create tension.

The result is a conflict between on one hand what projects should be, the criteria used to recruit project managers, the training they receive and the tools they use, and on the other what happens in the real world. The work of a good project manager differs from the training they receive. Good project managers are often good at their job, not because they adhere to the project model, but despite the model: good project managers often diverge from the project model.

```
   Project Model        →  ←  Observed Software Development
```

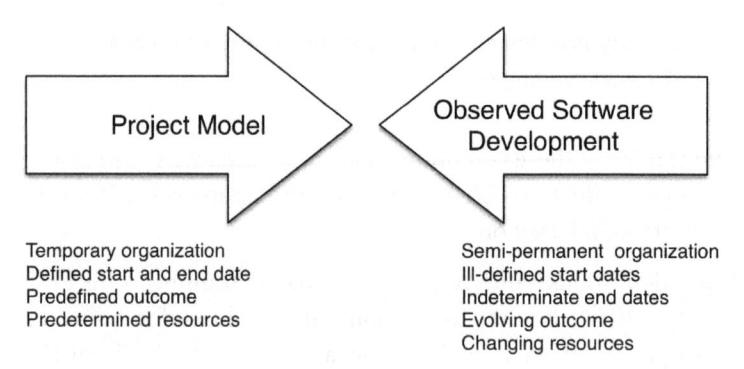

Temporary organization
Defined start and end date
Predefined outcome
Predetermined resources

Semi-permanent organization
Ill-defined start dates
Indeterminate end dates
Evolving outcome
Changing resources

Ideas underlying project management are in conflict with the realities of software development

Intelligent individuals who hold project management roles get put in impossible positions. Their training and professional institutions, their employer, its processes and structure can conflict with the right actions. Is it any wonder that project managers get a bad press when placed in such conflicted positions?

To return to the football parallel I drew earlier, what if the referee and officials were using Australian Rules or the Gaelic Football rule book? It is not just project managers who encounter tension between what a project should be and what it frequently is.

Maybe the people called 'project managers' would be better termed 'development managers'. In which case, why not train such people to manage software development? Why not give them a mental model that works, rather than a flawed model?

Many project managers bring experience and skills to a software development effort. Development efforts require work that is not coding and testing, and such managers can help. Each individual should be judged on their own skills and experience, but to recruit people with reference to an incorrect model and then ask them to make the model fit is to invite failure. (Interestingly, the title *Delivery Manager* is used increasingly instead of *Project Manager*. This change might be a reflection of exactly this issue.)

The word 'project' does not have universal meaning. Perhaps because the traditional project model is such a bad fit for software development, our industry has developed multiple meanings for the term.

4.7 Definitions of success

The lack of common meaning and abuse of the project model creates greater tension. With different definitions come different success criteria, which in turn imply different courses of action and outcomes. For example:

- If a project is defined by the source codebase then success may mean longevity and code quality; failure would mean code nobody wanted to work on.
- If a project is a stream of ongoing work, then success means happy customers and continued investment; failure would be falling customer numbers and reduced investment.
- If a project is a value-seeking team working on a business opportunity, success is measured by value delivered and improved business processes or products; failure would be recurring costs greater than the returned value.

So how one defines a 'project' determines how one assesses success and failure. When different team members use different definitions there is no shared goal and no shared definition of success.

4.8 In conclusion

If any project aficionado has read this far they may well be screaming "You are talking about product-oriented companies!" Educated project managers recognize an alternative model of an ongoing product that does not conform to the project model. They are right: the world I describe is a product world, but... The project model has become *de rigueur* in organizations, and gets applied almost universally: even organizations that recognize themselves as product operations employ project managers.

Many organizations and teams are already beyond projects, but in doing *false projects* they retain the language, paraphernalia and fripperies of projects – such as employees with the title of *Project Manager*. Here the projects model complicates straight thinking. Removing the language and model actually simplifies reasoning and managing.

Some might dismiss these arguments as 'word games', but I think Wittgenstein has a point. Language shapes thinking and action. Philosophers use the term *performativity* to describe how language influences action. When different people are using the same words to mean different things, their actions will differ in ways others will find hard to understand.

Thus the first problem with projects is that individuals do not necessarily agree on what a project is. Indeed, the use of the same word, but meaning different things, undoubtedly contributes to part of the problem of misaligned goals.

For the purposes of this book I follow the project management definitions, and specifically the idea that *projects have end dates*. This idea in itself is corrosive and damaging to the software engineering profession and the software industry.

5. Diseconomies of scale

> *Whenever a theory appears to you as the only possible one, take this as a sign that you have neither understood the theory nor the problem which it was intended to solve.* Karl Popper, philosopher, 1902-1994

Without really thinking about it, you are not only familiar with the idea of economies of scale – you expect economies of scale. Much of our market economy operates on the assumption that when you buy or spend more, you get more per unit of spending. The assumption of economies of scale is not confined to free-market economies: the same assumption underlays much communist era planning.

At some stage in our education – even if you never studied economics or operational research – you will have assimilated the idea that if Henry Ford builds a million identical black cars and sells a million cars, then each car will cost less than if Henry Ford manufactures one car, sells one car, builds another very similar car, sells that car, and continues in the same way another 999,998 times.

The net result is that Henry Ford produces cars more cheaply and sells more cars more cheaply, so buyers benefit. This is *economies of scale.*

The idea and history of mass production and economies of scale are intertwined. I'm not discussing mass production here, I'm talking *economies of scale* and *diseconomies of scale*.

5.1 Milk is cheaper in large cartons

That economies of scale exist is common sense: every day one experiences situations in which buying more of something is cheaper per unit than buying less. For example, you expect that in your local supermarket buying one large carton of milk – say four pints – will be cheaper than buying four one-pint cartons.

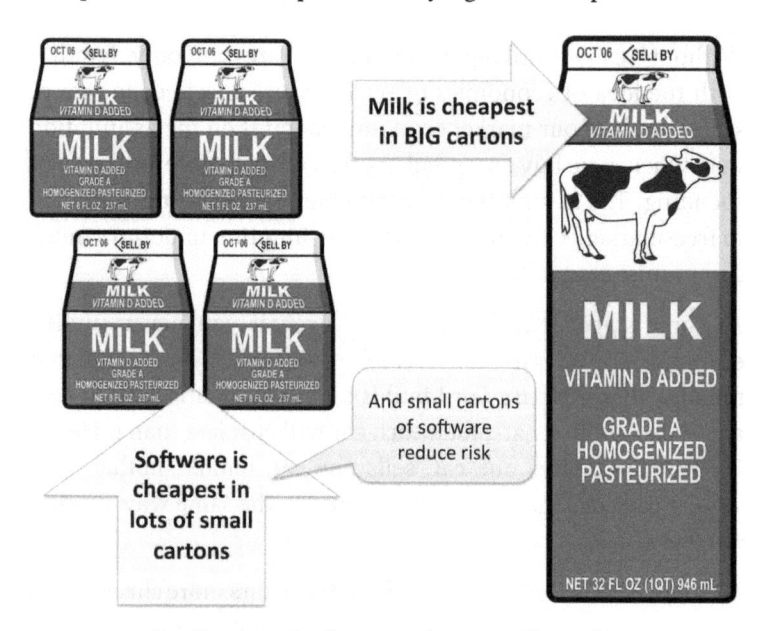

Small cartons of software are cheaper and less risky

So ingrained is this idea that it is newsworthy if shops charge more per unit for larger packs – complaints are made. In April 2015 *The Guardian* newspaper in London ran this story:

> *UK supermarkets dupe shoppers out of hundreds of millions, says Which?*
>
> Examples raised by Which? include Tesco flagging the 'special value' of a six-pack of sweetcorn when a smaller pack was proportionately cheaper, and Asda raising the individual price of a product when it was part of a multi-buy offering in order to make the deal more attractive[1].

Economies of scale are often cited as the reason for corporate mergers. Buying more allows buyers to extract price concessions from suppliers. Manufacturing more allows the cost per unit to be reduced, and such savings can be passed on to buyers if they buy more. Purchasing departments expect economies of scale.

I am not for one minute arguing that economies of scale do not exist: in some industries economies of scale are very real. Milk production and retail are examples. It is reasonable to assume such economies exist in most mass-manufacturing domains, and they are clearly present in marketing and branding.

But... and this is a big 'but'...

> *Software development does not have economies of scale*

---

[1] *UK supermarkets dupe shoppers out of hundreds of millions, says Which?*, 21 April 2015, https://www.theguardian.com/business/2015/apr/21/uk-supermarkets-dupe-shoppers-out-of-hundreds-of-millions-says-which

Diseconomies of scale

In all sorts of ways, software development has diseconomies of scale. If software development was sold by the pint, then a four-pint carton of software would not just cost four times the price of a one-pint carton, it would cost *far more*.

Once software is built there are massive economies of scale in reselling (and reusing) the same software and services built on it. Producing the first piece of software has massive marginal costs; producing the second, identical copy, has a cost so close to zero it is unmeasurable – Ctrl-C, Ctrl-V.

Diseconomies abound in the world of software development. Once development is complete, once the marginal costs of one copy are paid, then economies of scale dominate, because marginal cost is as close to zero as to make no difference.

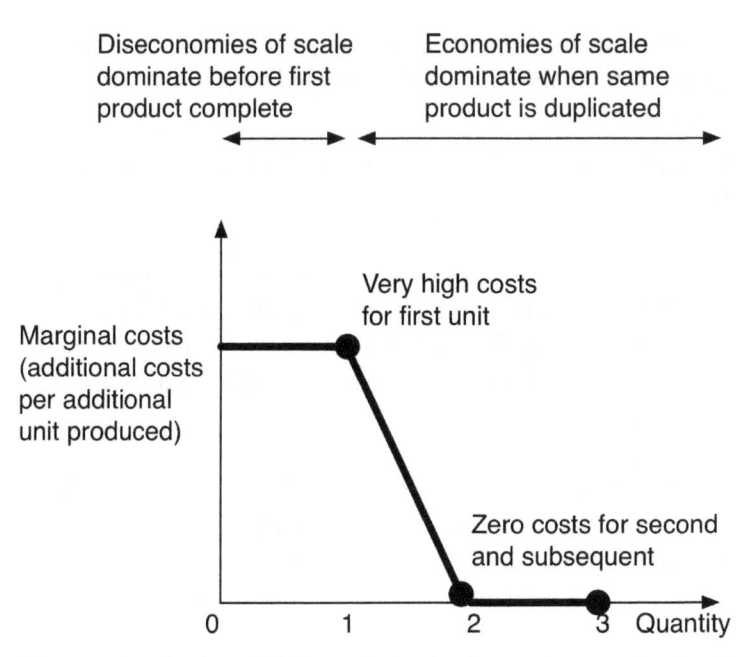

Diseconomies of scale and high marginal costs give way to economies of scale and negligible marginal costs

5.2 Evidence of diseconomies

Software development diseconomies of scale have been observed for some years. Cost estimation models like COCOMO actually include an adjustment for diseconomies of scale. But the implications of diseconomies are rarely factored into management thinking – rather, economies of scale thinking prevails.

Small development teams frequently outperform large teams; five people working as a tight team will be far more productive per person than a team of 50, or even 15. The Quattro Pro development team in the early 1990s is probably the best-documented example of this[2].

A more recent study of open source software development states that:

> 'We find strong evidence for a negative relation between team size and productivity. ...we further conclude that all of the studied projects represent diseconomies of scale, exhibiting diminishing returns to scale[3]'.

The more lines of code a piece of software has, the more difficult it is to add an enhancement or fix a bug. Putting a fix into a system with a million lines of code can easily be more than ten times harder than fixing a system with 100,000 lines.

As much as software engineers love the Lego-brick analogy, software does not scale like Lego. Software exhibits power-law characteristics[4]. Some parts of the system become more central. They are connected to more parts and changed far more often. Making multiple simultaneous changes to these parts is difficult, so changes must be sequenced. Consequently bringing more people to bear on the code does not make change happen faster – it happens more slowly.

---

[2] *Organizational Patterns of Agile Software Development*, Coplien & Harrison, 2005.

[3] *From Aristotle to Ringelmann: a Large-scale Analysis of Team Productivity and Coordination in Open Source Software projects*, Scholtes, Mavrodiev, Schweitzer, Empirical Software Engineering volume 21 issue 2, April 2016, pre-print version available https://www.sg.ethz.ch/media/publication_files/paper_bQeEC8G.pdf

[4] *Understanding the Shape of Java Software*, Gareth J Baxter, James Noble, Marcus Frean and Ewan D. Tempero, Proceedings of the 21th Annual ACM SIGPLAN Conference on Object-Oriented Programming, Systems, Languages, and Applications, OOPSLA 2006, October 22-26, 2006, Portland, Oregon, USA

Experience of *work in progress* limits shows that doing less at any one time gets more done overall.

Projects that set out to be *big* have far higher costs and lower productivity per deliverable unit than small systems. Capers Jones' 2008 book contains some tables of productivity per function point that illustrate this. It is worth noting that the biggest systems are usually military, and they have an atrocious productivity rate, not to mention horrendous schedule slips. The Airbus A400 transport was reportedly four years late and €5 billion over budget, while the Lockheed F35 fighter is reportedly seven years late and $163 billion over budget[5].

Testing

Testing is another area where diseconomies of scale play out. Testing a piece of software with two changes requires more tests, time and money than the sum of testing each change in isolation.

When two changes are tested together the combination of both changes needs to be tested as well. As more changes are added and more tests are needed, there is a combinatorial explosion in the number of test cases required, and thus a greater than proportional change in the time and money needed to undertake the tests. But testing departments regularly lump multiple changes together for testing in an effort to exploit economies of scale. In attempting to exploit non-existent economies of scale, testing departments increase costs, risks and time needed.

If a test should find a bug that needs to be fixed, finding the offending code in a system that has fewer changes is far easier

---

[5]https://en.wikipedia.org/wiki/Lockheed_Martin_F-35_Lightning_II#Program_cost_-overruns_and_delays

than finding and fixing a bug when there are more changes to be considered.

Working on larger endeavors means waiting longer – and probably writing more code – before you ask for feedback or user validation compared to smaller endeavors. As a result, there is more that could be 'wrong', more that users don't like, more spent, more that needs changing and more to complicate the task of applying fixes.

Cost of delay

Waiting is an interesting case because it has a cost. The longer it takes to deliver a product, the greater the *cost of delay*[6]. For example, the more time the product spends in development, the greater the costs, the more time it spends in development, the less time it spends in the market, the less time it is in the market before competitors arrive, and so on.

(To my mind *cost of delay* would be better called *benefit foregone* or *value foregone*.)

Those who have worked on agile teams that use small stories, or user stories, will have noticed that small stories flow through the system and are delivered sooner than large stories. For this reason agile teams often want lots of small stories rather than fewer larger stories. Unfortunately they are often met by product managers who claim that "The customer wants all or nothing. The customer will not accept anything less than everything they asked for."

---

[6] *The Principles of Product Development Flow*, Don Reinertsen, Celerita Publishing 2009.

Cost of delay means that delivering something sooner, even if it is smaller, may well be worth more than delivering a big thing later. Even if creating the big thing enjoys economies of scale – which is doubtful – and is cheaper per unit (line of code?) than a small thing, the revenue lost because of late delivery needs to be considered.

Batch size

Software development works best in small batch sizes. There are a few places where software development does exhibit economies of scale in which case large batch sizes make sense, but on most occasions, diseconomies of scale are the norm. (Reinertsen[7] has some figures on batch size that also support the diseconomies of scale argument.)

This happens because each time you add to software work the marginal cost per unit increases:

- Add a fourth team member to a team of three and the communication paths increase from three to six.
- Add one feature to a release and you have one feature to test; add two features and you have three tests to run: two features to test plus the interaction between the two.

In part this is because human minds can only hold so much complexity. As the complexity increases (more changes, more code) our cognitive load increases, mental processing slows down, people make more mistakes and work takes longer.

---
[7] *The Principles of Product Development Flow*, Don Reinertsen, Celerita Publishing 2009.

Economies of scope and specialization are specific forms of economies of scale and again, on the whole, software development has diseconomies of scope and diseconomies of specialization:

- Teams should focus first and broaden later when they have a working product.
- Generalists are usually preferable to specialists: technologies that demand in-depth expertise should be avoided if possible.

However, be careful: once the software is developed then economies of scale are rampant. The world switches. Software that has been built probably exhibits more economies of scale than any other product known to man.

(In economic terms the marginal cost of producing the first instance are extremely high, but the marginal costs of producing an identical copy (production) are so close to zero as to be zero, Ctrl-C Ctrl-V.)

5.3 Think diseconomies, think small

First of all you need to rewire your brain: almost everyone in the advanced world has been brought up with economies of scale since school. You need to start thinking *diseconomies of scale*.

Second, whenever faced with a problem where you feel the urge to 'go bigger', run in the opposite direction: go smaller.

Third, take each and every opportunity to go small.

Fourth, get good at working 'in the small': optimize your processes, tools and approaches to do lots of small things rather than a few big things.

Fifth – and this is the killer: know that most people don't get this at all. In fact, it's worse...

5.4 Economies of scale thinking prevails

In any existing organization, particularly a large corporation, the majority of people who make decisions are out and out economies of scale thinkers. They expect that going big is cheaper than going small and they force this view on others, especially software technology people.

Many senior people got to where they are today because of economies of scale, and many of these companies exist because of economies of scale; if they are good at economies of scale, they are good at doing what they do.

Consider banking for example. Banking, both retail and investment, exhibits many economies of scale. These occur in marketing: the same brand can offer many services and cross-sell: sign a customer for a current account, later sell them a loan, then a mortgage, then life insurance and so on.

Economies of scale occur in capital funding too. Some have even argued that size alone, while making banks riskier, also makes their funding cheaper, because governments must underwrite 'too big to fail banks'[8].

There are those who claim that modern banks are disguised software companies. Yet the individuals who reach positions of authority in a bank will do so because they are good bankers rather than good technologists. Consequently they will have spent a career exploiting economies of scale thinking. When confronted with technology concerns they will cling to what has brought success in the past: economies of scale. Inevitably this will place them in conflict when faced with a problem that requires the opposite thinking.

In the world of software development this mindset is a recipe for failure and underperformance. The conflict between economies of scale thinking and diseconomies of scale working will create tension and conflict.

5.5 And projects...

Part of the problem with projects is that they are, almost by definition, large batches of work. The administrative work involved in creating a project, getting it approved, bringing the resources together, making the resources work together effectively, then at the end unwinding all the temporary structures means that the project model only makes sense when projects are large.

Complicating matters, it can be hard to disentangle the costs of the organization from actual development costs. Some organizations demand that all work is conducted under the project model; consequently, whether the initiative is small or large, two

---

[8] *The Bankers New Clothes*, Admati & Hellwig, 2013

weeks of effort or two years, both initiatives require the same preparation, paperwork and approval.

In the language of economists, both initiatives have fixed costs (the start-up costs), but the longer initiative will have lower average costs. This is because the same fixed start-up costs are amortized over more production units. However, because the larger initiative requires more coordination, the marginal costs per unit will be higher. Consequently it can be hard to do true cost comparisons between endeavors.

Companies seem to like projects: projects imply change, and change implies growth. This is much more attractive than 'business as usual'. But the need for projects to be large means small is not an option, and therefore the stakes are high and the risks are large.

Unfortunately, software development lacks economies of scale. Time and time again building software in the small is more efficient than doing so in the large.

> *Software is cheapest in small quantities.*

There is an inherent conflict between the best way of running a project and the best way of organizing software development endeavors.

5.6 Making small decisions

In part big-batch projects are an attempt to maximize the value of the most precious limited resource: senior management time. Getting time with a senior manager is difficult, their interest in discussing anything worth less than $10 million is negligible (replace with a relevant figure for your organization). So why bother them with small pieces of work? You are more likely to get a few minutes of their time to approve a $10 million project than to discuss 100 small $100,000 pieces of work.

For software development to exploit the rampant diseconomies of scale, decision authority needs to be devolved downwards so that small decisions can be made efficiently when needed, rather than bundled into single big decisions.

5.7 Optimize for small

Diseconomies of scale mean that organizational structures need to be reconsidered. Individuals, teams and organizations need to learn to think small. They need to start looking for *small*:

> Teams need to organize themselves for lots of small.

> Organizations, teams, processes and practices need to be optimized for small.

Because of diseconomies of scale, it is necessary to rethink the traditional economies of scale-based organizational structures, and create structures and processes that are optimized for small. Only by optimizing for small can organizations and team exploits diseconomies of scale.

Work processes need to be optimized for small pieces of work – small batch sizes and small items. This means big activities (for example set-up, teardown, one-off reviews) need to be removed.

Things that are expensive and get minimized (such as sign-off and final test cycles) need to be removed or rethought so that they can be efficient in the small.

Each of those small pieces of work needs to demonstrate potential value and be evaluated later for value delivered.

5.8 Kelly's Laws

I have two personal laws.

Kelly's first law of project complexity

> *Project scope will always increase in proportion to resources.*

The more people, time, and money you have, the more your project will attempt to do.

Kelly's second law of project complexity

> *Inside every large project there is a small one struggling to get out.*

Look for the small piece of work struggling to get out, then work to deliver that early.

6. Software isn't temporary

Let's look again at those definitions of what a project is:

> The PMI (Project Management Institute) defines a project by its two key characteristics: it is temporary and undertaken to create a product, service, or result that is unique.

And the PRINCE2 handbook – a UK Government-sponsored standard – contains the following definition of a project:

> 'A temporary organization that is needed to produce a unique and predefined outcome or result at a pre-specified time using predetermined resources'

It is the temporary idea that underlies the project model that causes Project Myopia and many of the resulting problems. This short-sighted model has been foisted onto software engineers. The problem is that projects are intended for temporary endeavors.

The key characteristic of any projects is that it ends. However software doesn't end: software that is successful continues to change long after its original delivery date.

There are true project temporary endeavors out there. I don't claim to know much about construction or manufacturing, so projects might well exist there. But I do claim to know a lot about software engineering and businesses built on software technology – what we call 'digital' today.

When software has users and gets used there will be requests to change it: requests to fix problems, enhance the software and update it for changing business problems. As users learn and change, the business will also learn and change, so the software must 'learn' and change too.

As we observed in the opening chapters of this book, modern twenty-first century growth businesses are overwhelmingly digital. Software powers these growth business. Software creation and enhancement isn't a temporary thing they do at the beginning and forget about: it *is* the business.

Software almost lives, in the same way that animals live and businesses live. One day it may end, die, the same way that animals die. Businesses die too, although they might try hard to avoid their fate. By imposing an end date the project model tries to kill software. But when the software is beneficial, when people want the software, then it breaks the project model. End dates get missed, or a new project appears to manage the changes requested.

Long-lived software will need to be moved ('ported') to new technologies: new operating systems, new databases, new processors and new devices. Software is build on infrastructure, and when that changes the software needs to change too. Stop the software changing and you stop the business evolving and growing.

How much software that was never supposed to change again continues to change? Introduction of the Euro and the Y2K problem 19 years ago saw millions of lines of old code examined and changed. How much of this 'finished' software is still in use today? How much of it is still changing?

Software is part of our infrastructure. Government social security systems and bank payment systems are the bridges and highways of the modern world. The world changes and our software must change.

For physical infrastructure there is often a clear differentiation between construction and subsequent maintenance. In software this boundary is far from clear-cut; it is easy to move requests between the two. Also, as this book will argue, some of the practices used to bring software 'construction' to a close adversely effect the subsequent maintenance activity.

Visit SourceForge, look at the products that get the most downloads: they also have recent changes applied. Look at the software that nobody downloads: in most cases it won't have changed for months or years. Software that gets used demands change.

The only software that doesn't change is dead software.

Stopping software from changing is a fast way to kill it.

Treating software development as a temporary endeavor kills it.

Considering software as a temporary artifact means that the teams that create it get regarded as temporary too. Teams get disbanded at 'the end'. Its developers scatter to the four winds, and with them the shared understanding and knowledge of how the software works. This means that knowledge of how to change the software gets lost.

Disbanding high-performing teams is worse than vandalism: it is *corporate psychopathy*.

When project aficionados acknowledge that a software product will need to change in future, they exchange one myopia for another. They are likely to insist that documentation should form part of the delivered artifacts. There is a belief that written words will allow others to change the software in the future. But documentation doesn't work.

Documentation is a very poor way of capturing and communicating knowledge – especially the tacit knowledge that is vital when trying to understand and change software. Documentation frequently diverges from what the actual code base does, especially when documentation is written in advance of the software. When documentation gets written – at a cost that may exceed that of the actual code itself – it is frequently never read.

Even when someone does read it, very little of the original message is received, and even less retained. When starting a new programming position I was sometimes handed a pile of documentation on my first day in a new role. I would wade through with the aid of a lot of coffee, but very little was ever retained in my head.

Although project managers and corporations run a mental model of temporary teams, such teams are often kept together in defiance of the project model. While this is good – it at least retains tacit knowledge – it creates conflicts. Conflict arises because the model – and the business assumptions built on the model – is different than 'the real world'. The real world doesn't follow the project model!

While officially a temporary endeavor, in practice one temporary project begets another temporary project, which begets another, and so on. The resulting 'temporary' but not actually temporary project creates tension and conflict.

Ironically, deadlines are useful: deadlines are a great way of organizing work, creating focus and motivating people. However, artificial end dates positioned at unnatural times damage software quality.

Rather than ask "How long will this take?", ask "What is the date of maximum value?" and then "What can we build to capture as much of that value as possible?". Effort estimation may have a role in the discussion, but it is secondary to business imperatives. Business dates should drive work, not effort estimates.

7. If they use it, it will change

> *The most loved and legendary building of all at MIT is a surprise: a temporary building left over from World War II without even a name, only a number: Building 20. ...constructed hastily in 1943 for urgent development of radar and almost immediately slated for demolition.* Stewart Brand[1], author

> *Building 55 was demolished in 1998, 55 years after its construction.*

When preparing one of the earliest #NoProjects presentations – for the *BCS Project Management Special Interest Group*, no less – I set out to prove a direct correlation between software use and changes to a software code base.

SourceForge, the massive open source repository, provides a great data source for examining this hypothesis. I reasoned that if people downloaded software, then they had an interested in the software. Not every download might result in an install, not every install might result in use and not every user might become a regular user, but it was good enough.

First I looked at Moodle[2]. SourceForge describes this as:

---

[1] *How Building Learn*, Stewart Brand, 1994
[2] https://sourceforge.net/projects/moodle

> 'A Course Management System (CMS), also known as a Learning Management System (LMS) or a Virtual Learning Environment (VLE). It is a free web application that educators can use to create effective online learning sites.'

On the 19 January 2014 I noted that:

- In the previous week Moodle had 23,239 downloads.
- The last code change to Moodle was 16 January, only three days before my search.

Moodle was clearly of interest to people, and if only 1% of those downloads resulted in an active user that was still 232 new users in the last week. Moodle was living and changing.

Then I looked, almost at random, at PerlLord[3]:

> 'Web wrapper for the upcoming release of LORD/x – a Linux version of LORD, the classic BBS game from way back. This program converts ANSI to HTML (Yes, HTML, not GIF or JPEG) So you can actually play in a browser'.

In the week leading up to 19 January 2014 there had been precisely zero downloads of this software. The last code change was in April 2013, nine months previously.

Certainly someone out there might still be using PerlLord, but it wasn't growing and it wasn't changing.

One more. I found a thing called WebTorrent[4]:

---
[3] https://sourceforge.net/projects/perllord
[4] https://sourceforge.net/projects/web-torrent/

> 'WebTorrent is a web-based GUI written in Python for the Bit Torrent Library. It is designed for server applications where installation of desktop bt (sic) clients are not feasible'.

Again no downloads in the preceding week, and no changes for over eight months.

Writing now in December 2016:, nearly three years later:

- Moodle had 1,220 downloads in the previous week and the last code update was two days ago.
- PerLord has had no downloads this week and no updates since early 2013[5].
- WebTorrent has had no downloads this week either, although an update happened 10 months ago, so there is some interest.

That someone changed WebTorrent implies someone was, even is, using it. With no downloads recorded one might reason that that someone was its creator, for whom WebTorrent fills a need. Someone uses it, someone changes it, but it is not a growth market.

In fact there were no downloads of either PerlLord or WebTorrent at all in the intervening years. Moodle on the other hand had nearly 900,000 downloads. (Although downloads fell drastically after August 2018, which suggests something significant happened about then.)

Clearly WebTorrent and PerlLord are dead and do not change.

---

[5] Oddly the last update seems earlier than my previous check, so maybe a change was rolled back.

Moodle lives. Not only do thousands of instance of Moodle exist, but it has itself divided amoeba-like – or 'forked', to use the correct open source terminology – with the creation of Totara and possibly other versions I do not know of.

7.1 Counter-argument

The above analysis is weak because it rests on a small sample of only three applications. So let's make a note to undertake a more rigorous study in the near future, but in the meantime let's pretend this study is valid.

The analysis is also weak because correlation does not prove causation. Are these phenomena independent or is there cause-and-effect? And if so, which is cause and which is effect?

Let's take them one at a time.

Commercial parallel

The open source examples parallel what happens in the world of commercial software: companies produce software; if the software sells the company invests more in the software and produces new versions to sell to new customers, and equally important, to sell to their existing customers.

In fact this is the business model of what used to be called 'independent software vendors', companies such as Microsoft, Oracle, Corel, Borland, JD Edwards, Sage, SAP and so on. Selling software again to existing customers is a key element of this business model. Once a software vendor has a customer, then selling them a second piece of software or an upgrade is easier:

customers are an asset. (Several of the patterns in *Business Patterns for Software Developers* deal explicitly with this model, for example *Same Customer, Different Product*.)

A big part of the struggle for start-up software vendors is securing those initial customer who provide recurring revenue. In the extreme these customers are captive – have you ever tried getting a company to change an ERP system?

Conversely, software vendors who cannot get users (that is, sales) go out of business. Consider Corel and the old Borland: as customers stopped using WordPerfect and Turbo Pascal sales fell, there was less money for investment, which made it more difficult to keep up with competitors whose products became more attractive. Certainly there were other forces at work, but the update cycle was an important part of what happened.

It is Darwinian. Usage drives sales and sales drive usage, but to keep the treadmill operating new features and functionality must be introduced to oil the machinery. With no software changes there is no reason to buy (again), and thus no sales and no revenue. Sooner or later no revenue means no company.

If there was no cause-and-effect relationship between software changes and usage there would not be a software industry as we know it. Microsoft, Oracle, Fog Creek and others would not exist. Since they do exist the logic of the market forces demands that changes and usage are related.

When a software vendor sells products on subscription, as Microsoft does with Office 365, customers need to keep paying even if there are no changes. However, if Microsoft did not keep changing and enhancing the software competitors would catch up and start stealing customers.

Cause and effect?

If changes to the software create demand for the software – that is, open source downloads or commercial sales – then ceasing to change the software blunts demand.

If demand for the software drives change – people using the software request changes – then declining change requests leaves an unmet demand. Those making the request get frustrated and potential business value is foregone. For example, process optimizations are passed over and enhanced customer satisfaction opportunities ignored. Over time this will create a class of underserved users and customers and an opportunity for disruptive innovation[6].

Consider Microsoft Office

A combination of these forces forced the mighty Microsoft to change direction for Office (Word, Excel, PowerPoint) when Apple iPads and iPhones became popular. At first Microsoft held back from producing Word, Excel and the rest of Office for Apple iOS. But customers wanted the new Apple technology and the lack of Microsoft products did not deter them.

As it happened Microsoft Office over-served much of its market. Many customers would have been happy to buy less functional products for less money. But because Microsoft Office dominated the market there was little competition. In addition, network effects mean that while Microsoft Office is dominant anyone not using Office will be at a disadvantage.

---

[6] *The Innovator's Dilemma*, Christensen, C.M., 1997

By not advancing their own software, Microsoft allowed EverNote and Apple's own software (Pages, Numbers and Keynote) to become established. Now there were viable competitors. At the same time the network effects reduced because more people were using other products.

Eventually Microsoft had little choice but to port Office to iOS. Had they not done so Office would have lost dominance in the market.

7.2 Conclusion

One might argue that the dynamics of open source commercial software packages and in-house bespoke software means that conclusions drawn about one type of software do not apply to others. That argument has some merit, but at the end of the day those who pay – customers who choose – can choose between software following different commercial models. All three types complete with each other. Some lessons cross commercial models.

> *Only dead software stops changing.*

> *Why force software to stop changing? Killing software changes eschews benefit.*

When considering changes to software the benefit they bring to the business needs to be considered, rather than the cost of making the changes or arbitrary deadlines.

Project Myopia strikes again: by forcing closure the project model kills changes and kills software.

Viewing software as an asset, a living asset at that, an asset that increases in value, shows how shortsighted the project approach is.

8. False projects

Many teams work not so much on projects as *false projects*. These are development endeavors that use the language of projects but do not follow the project model. Language that should bring shared understanding brings conflict and confusion.

False projects manifest themselves as one project followed by another project with the same personnel, working on the same code base and hence the same technology and the same domain. A second project follows the first, a third follows the second and so forth. Some teams spend years rolling from one project to another in this fashion.

At one organization I had the following discussion:

> Me: "What happens if the project does not meet all its aims?"
>
> Project Manager: "Anything important gets rolled to the next project"
>
> Me: "Is another project planned?"
>
> Project Manager: "Yes, all projects start on April 1st"

The organization had aligned its project cycles with the financial year. Each financial year contained a collection of projects.

While this is undoubtedly one approach, it is not necessarily an effective one.

So teams are almost applying an agile-style fix iteration length with variable scope model. An iteration length of one year is exceptional. The project dressing makes it hard to discern what the business objective is.

Nor is the problem confined to aligning projects with financial accounting years. Companies, even product companies, know they must continually update their product, but these updates happen as a series of projects. The language of the project model, and even the role of project manager, aggrandize what should be business as usual.

False projects are a problem because they are neither one thing or another, so *how does one judge success?* They maintain the trapping and mindset of projects in what is not in honesty a project environment. As a result they obscure reality, they hinder system thinking and hence improvement.

9. The problem with project success

Consider the well known troika of success for projects:

- On-schedule delivery
- On-budget delivery
- On-quality delivery

Think about this list of criteria: can you see identify a problem with them?

This particular project success troika dominates project thinking. But something is missing: value. These 'success' criteria do not consider the importance of the value created by the project.

Value is usually taken to mean dollars, euros, sterling, a hard number. However it is better to consider value more generally as *business benefit* – that is, the benefit delivered to the organization sponsoring the development effort.

Each development effort should be clear about what constitutes benefit to the organization. For commercial organizations the benefit may well be money, specifically profit measured in dollars, pounds or some other currency. Other measures of benefit are possible. For a charity it might be how many people have clean drinking water, for a hospital it might be lives saved, and for a school it could be attainment grades.

Strictly speaking the terms *value* and *benefit* are different: *value* implies a hard number, while *benefit* more readily encompasses non-financial outcomes. In general conversation the two are synonymous. Perhaps because people prefer a hard number, or perhaps because 'value' is shorter to write and say, 'value' is more common.

Those who worship at the altar of projects would have us believe that delivering on schedule, budget and quality will unlock the value promised by the project. After all, isn't that why a company requires a business case before work on the project can begin?

9.1 Project assumptions

Two assumptions underlie the project model and these criteria:

- Benefit is known before work commences (which implies the benefit is knowable in advance).
- There is little or no value in flexibility.

For the sake of brevity I will leave aside the question of how one knows what the value is and whether determining that benefit should have been part of the project in the first place.

In a world where computing power doubles every two years, where both technology and business are in a constant state of flux, and where every loft and garage seems to contain a disruptive start-up, is it really possible to know the benefit of work in advance? Ask yourself: before owning a smartphone, did you really understand the benefits of having email in your pocket? Or Facebook? Twitter? 24x7 news?

Before the advent of Uber I could get a taxi easily, but since Uber arrived it is even easier. That means that I use more taxis, which might be a benefit, but I end up spending more. Understanding the benefits and value of new technology without seeing and experiencing it is very difficult.

Projects set out to deliver predetermined functionality (scope) in a predetermined time with predetermined resources (that is, budget). However, the modern business environment is constantly changing. The tension between businesses' desire for predictability and the simultaneous demand for flexibility undermines teams and projects, thereby reducing the chances of success.

In fact one of the project success troika is itself ambiguous: *quality*. Some versions of the success troika say 'requested feature', while others say 'required quality'. Some people even equate quality with features, as if more features makes for better software. A discussion of software quality is worth an essay in its own right, but I must save that for another day.

But it gets worse.

9.2 Goal displacement

These assumptions – that benefit is known in advance and flexibility lacks value – lead to the definition of faulty success criteria. These simple concrete success criteria silently become the goal of the work rather than its original goal(s). When the true goals are intangible, hard to define, hard to attain and difficult to measure, it is more attractive to focus on the success troika: three hard, tangible, measurable goals.

Sociologist Robert Merton coined the term *goal displacement* to describe just this scenario. Rather than focus on the true goal of work – to deliver business benefit – projects focus on satisfying the success troika. People shelter behind these proxy aims and manage work towards the wrong goal. Organizations, processes and even job roles become oriented to deliver these lesser but tangible goals instead of higher-value intangible goals.

One shouldn't blame managers for this situation: all of us give in to goal displacement at times, even me. Rather than pursue the real goal, which might be difficult to achieve, people focus on some proxy. Unfortunately, in chasing the proxy they miss the real goal.

Back in 2006 Professor John Ward at Cranfield University in the UK published a survey of IT managers in the UK and Benelux countries (*Delivering Value from IS and IT Investments*). The survey's findings are most interesting:

- 70% of managers believed they were failing to identify and quantify the benefits adequately.
- 38% of managers openly admitted to overstating project benefits in order to obtain funding. (One has to wonder about the other 62% who because of their honesty are less likely to get their genuine projects funded.)
- 80% of managers reported that the review and evaluation of completed projects is also inadequate, due to the focus on whether the project achieved cost, time and quality objectives rather than on the realization of intended benefits.

The first two points are incriminating in their own right, but it is the third that proves the damage of traditional project success criteria: in effect 80% of managers see the traditional project success criteria as an obstacle.

While this survey was conducted over ten years ago, there seems little reason to believe that similar research today would find differently. Certainly anecdotal reports suggest that the situation is no better.

10. Multiple projects

Sometimes it is important to take a board view. It is when one looks more broadly that some problems with the project model become clearer. Specifically, when a company undertakes project after project after project, and when a team can deliver regularly – continuous-delivery style – then working across projects can increase the return on investment. But this comes at a price.

To do this one has to forego project success criteria. Working to maximize value does not sit well with meeting predetermined schedules, budgets and feature lists.

At best maintaining the project model is superfluous and creates extra work. At worst it sets up competing goals and causes confusion. To illustrate the conflicts, I've set up a small economic model.

10.1 A model

Let us assume a good agile team of four engineers. The team costs $10,000 a week to run. While each engineer probably earns a little over $100,000 per year, employers face additional costs in the form of benefits, desk space, paid vacation and so on.

The team is asked to undertake Project A. This project contains 12 independent work items, each of which will take one week to implement and release. The team works in business value order and starts with the most valuable item.

To compare scenarios I will use net present value, NPV. This is a well-known measure of the return on investment. To calculate NPV I also need to assume a discount rate, an interest rate.

The discount rate is important because money has its own price. A cash-rich company might choose to use existing reserves to build Project A, but in doing so the money is not doing something else. The same money could finance another project, or it could sit safely in a bank account earning interest.

Software developments are generally risky. Bank accounts are safe, US Government bonds even safer. So to justify a software project the return on investment must be higher. Companies need to balance their mix of cash and risk.

Conversely, a company short of cash might borrow the money. Borrowing usually comes at a higher interest rate. The rate varies massively depending on the lender, collateral posted, credit history and more.

At the time of writing the US Federal Reserve interest rate is 2%, so money safe in the bank doesn't earn much. But borrowing money costs a lot more. In evaluating any work companies should consider the funding model and alternative uses for the money.

For this model I'm assuming a 10% annual discount rate, which is 0.19% a week. As long as discount rates are positive the argument given here holds.

10.2 Project A

Project A is the simplest case. The team does the work and the revenue is recognized. After 12 weeks the company has spent

$120,000 but has earned $660,000. While it is tempting to say this means a 550% return on investment, that is untrue.

Project A	Value	Weeks	Cost	Net
A1	$120,000	1	$10,000	$110,000
A2	$110,000	1	$10,000	$100,000
A3	$100,000	1	$10,000	$90,000
A4	$90,000	1	$10,000	$80,000
A5	$80,000	1	$10,000	$70,000
A6	$70,000	1	$10,000	$60,000
A7	$60,000	1	$10,000	$50,000
A8	$50,000	1	$10,000	$40,000
A9	$40,000	1	$10,000	$30,000
A10	$30,000	1	$10,000	$20,000
A11	$20,000	1	$10,000	$10,000
A12	$10,000	1	$10,000	$0

Total cost = $120,000

Total net = $660,000

NPV = $654,537

To measure the return on investment one needs to consider the timing of cash flows. Money spent sooner costs more than money spent later.

In this model the money is not all spent at once and revenue does is not recognized in one event. This might be true in a traditional project in which all the money gets paid to a supplier on day one and all revenue is recognized on the last day.

A full NPV calculation values this work at $654,537. Still not bad, and not far off the naive calculation above. When the risk-free interest rate is higher, the difference is greater.

10.3 Project B

Now consider the team faced with two projects, A and B. For simplicity's sake both projects have the same profile of work items, effort and payback.

The team could choose to do Project A or Project B. Both would generate $660,000 in revenue and an NPV of $657,806.

The team decides to do Project A then Project B. For an outlay of $240,000 the company generates $1,320,000, an NPV of $1,294,156.

Notice the NPV for doing both projects in sequence is $15,000 less than simply adding A and B. This is because cash-flows occur over time. Higher discount rates mean that this difference would be larger.

For a team working under project management success criteria – deliver all features within budget and schedule – this makes sense. Both A and B could succeed. But this does not maximize value: there are at least two other options that could increase the value returned.

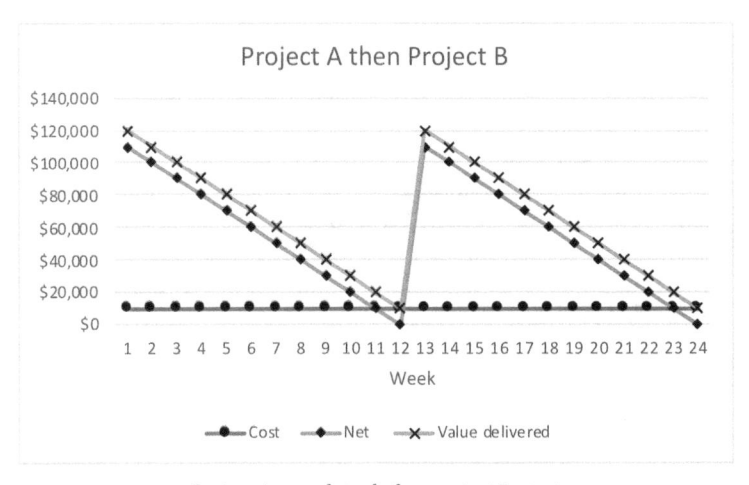

Project A completes before project B starts

10.4 Interleave A and B

If instead the team ignores the project boundary and cherry-picks high-value work from both projects, the total NPV will increase. For example, item A1 valued at $120,000 from Project A, then the similarly valued B1 from Project B, then the $110,000 A2 item from A and so on.

Now the total NPV from both projects rises to $1,299,521, an increase of $5,364. Although relatively small, this illustrates the point, and again with a higher discount rate the difference would increase.

Projects interleaved

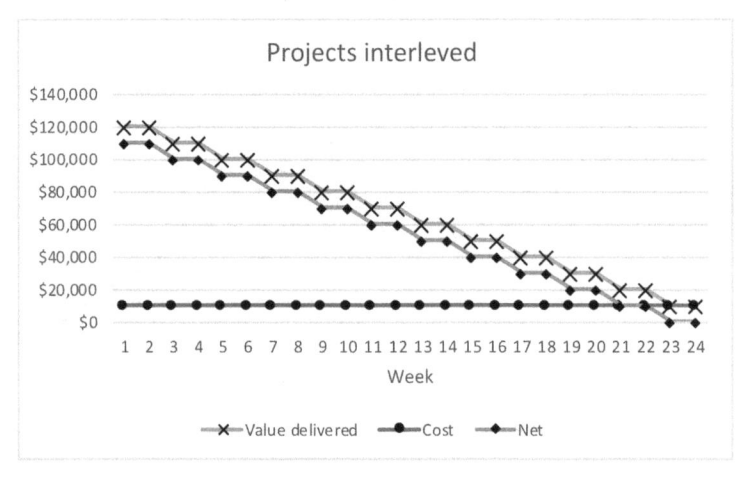

Projects interleaved

However, to interleave work the team needs to break project success criteria. Project A will now finish in 24 weeks rather than 12. Project B stakeholders may be happy to receive their requests sooner, but Project A stakeholders are likely to complain.

Strictly speaking, since Project B was originally scheduled to deliver second before the team decided to interleave them, then Project B would also break project success criteria. Projects that deliver early also trigger exception reports. Those working in IT see projects deliver early so seldom that many don't know this.

10.5 Split the team

Another alternative approach would be to split the team in two and have two sub-teams. Each sub-team would contain two engineers and they would work in parallel. To model this some tweaks are needed to the model.

This scenario produces an NPV of $1,298,047. While $3,891 higher than delivering A then B in sequence, this option is only $1,473 higher than interleaving the work. Again, while these numbers may be small, it still illustrate the point. (And rate rise.)

One might argue that with the difference so small other factors should be considered. For example, would the team still be as productive if split in two? Wold the risk profile change?

Then there is the question of management overhead. So far I have assumed that each option entails the same amount of time from people outside the team – preferably zero. But now there are two teams, each with its own delivery schedule, it is entirely possible that more management time needs to be devoted to the work.

10.6 Enter Project C

So far the analysis has focused on just two discrete projects. Yet, as this book argues, in reality software is a series of sequential changes. It just so happens that companies use the project model to divide work.

Consider for a moment that a third project, Project C, appears. Assume Project C has the same work/value profile as the previous two.

To meet project success criteria, Projects A and B need to be completed before work on C starts. But obviously the high-value items of C are worth more than the low-value items of A and B.

If A and B are interleaved then at almost any point work items can be pulled from C and the total NPV for a given period will increase. But this is only possible if the team breaks from the project model.

Splitting one of the sub-teams further into two could work, as would having one sub-team switch to Project C. One problem here is that because each sub-team takes longer to complete a work item, switching costs will be higher. Either work on Project C will need to wait while a sub-team completes a piece of work, or a sub-team will have to halt work that is only partially done.

In fact, not doing the last two items in both projects make no difference to NPV. Because in all projects the lowest value work items carry $10,000 value and the teams cost $10,000 a week to run, canceling these items will have no effect on NPV. However, releasing the team from A and B early allows them to do other valuable work.

10.7 What does this illustrate?

There are three lessons from this example.

First, picking high-value work from across projects increases value delivered rather than staying within a project. But in doing so the project breaks traditional success criteria. Maximizing value and meeting project goals are incompatible.

Second, teams need to be able to optimize their own performance. Teams are in the best position to analyze what they have been asked to do and decide for themselves on the best course of action. As the split-team option shows, sometimes decisions can be finely balanced.

Finally, having your own mental model of how to maximize value and organize teamwork opens up options. Having only one model in your mind, the project model, constrains options and thinking.

10.8 Assumptions

To make this model work I've had to make some assumptions:

- The team is well practiced at agile and work is packaged as a series of work items or stories that are independent of one another. So the project is truly a collection of work.
- The team is capable of building and releasing each item independently.
- Each work item is of similar size, complexity and risk.
- No additional resources outside of the teams are required. In particular, no additional management work is needed.
- No allowance is made for risk or for learning as the work proceeds – that is, productivity and value delivered do not change.
- Expenditures are paid for as they occur until the time when the money is safe in the bank.
- Changing requirements do not delay work or change value or work items.
- Revenue is recognized as the work item is delivered. See cost of delay below for more discussion of this point.
- Teams are organized as stable units under a 'flow the work to the team' model. *Continuous Digital* describes this model in more detail.
- Team members are interchangeable: this is a fairly big, and perhaps unrealistic, assumption, but only really effects the split-team option. If a team cannot be split like this then the split-team option is not available.

- Team members only work on these projects and there are no unforeseen or random items to interrupt work.

You may, and should, question each of these assumptions, so it is worth spelling them out. Every assumption could be relaxed, but with each relaxation the model would become more complex.

Some of the parameters are easier to vary than others. Take engineering salary level. $130,000 might seem too much or too little to you. This can easily be changed, and while it might invalidate the financial logic of doing a piece of work, the model itself would still stand.

No estimates

This model does not rely on the ability of the team to give accurate estimates. The model assumes that each work item is one week. For modeling purposes that is all that is needed. A more complex model could allow for variable work lengths.

Estimates are a non-issue because the model can be viewed retrospectively. That is, I could say "A team has completed two projects, A and B, with these characteristics... in retrospect, how might they have increased value?".

Cost of delay

One big assumption that does deserve to be questioned is the recognition of value. This model assumes that all the value for a work item accrues when work is complete and release has occurred. It further assumes that the value is static and does not vary over time.

Some work items will certainly fulfill this profile. Others will not, but will generate value over a period of time. Some items will be time-dependent: if released in time for Christmas, say, they will generate a lot of value, but if released after Christmas will generate little.

In other words, the model is making no allowance for cost-of-delay. In truth, each item will have a time-value profile that shows value being recognized over time and varying with the date of introduction. See my *Little Book of Requirements and User Stories*[1] for more discussion of time-value profiles, and Don Reinertsen's *The Principles of Product Development Flow*[2] for cost of delay.

Adding cost of delay and a revenue recognition schedule to this model would significantly increase the complexity. Nor do I believe it would substantially alter the conclusion.

---
[1] *Little Book of Requirements and User Stories*, Allan Kelly, 2016
[2] *The Principles of Product Development Flow*, Don Reinertsen, Celerita Publishing 2009.

11. Increasing value

Agile software development focuses on the small. Agile aims to deliver lots of small increments rapidly.

One of the key techniques of agile software development is that of breaking work down. This is a learnable skill. Again and again the agile solution to tackling a request is to break it down into smaller items. Teams initially build Minimally Viable Products and Walking Skeletons. Epic stories get broken down into smaller stories, which are themselves broken down into tasks.

To someone of an agile mind being told "We need all or nothing, if we don't have the whole thing... everything on our list is a must" is like a red rag to a bull. Experience shows that almost everything is decomposable when looked at in the right way and with the right toolkit. The all-or-nothing cry is often made without anyone actually trying to decompose the work.

So look again at the thing that we call 'a project'. The aim of the project originators is to create value by delivering the project. Goal displacement occurs in the gap between value identification and delivery, because the goals of each activity are not the same as the overall goal:

- Success in value identification means identifying and communicating potential business value and then getting a delivery project launched.

- Success in delivery means satisfying the success troika of schedule, cost and quality.

Yet the overall goal is to deliver value to the business, customers and users.

The alternative is to bring these activities together in value-seeking teams. Even when identification and delivery are separate a value-seeking team can deliver higher value by flexing and revalidating scope.

Viewed through the lens of the agile software movement, a project is actually a number of units of work that will hopefully deliver value. Some of these work units might deliver value sooner and some later. Some may require more work and some less. Some deliver lots of value and some less. Some are time-dependent and lose value quickly, others are not – the value they generate remains the same whenever delivered.

In other words, a project is a large batch of things – lets call them 'features' – each of which should contribute towards value. Since the world is still in motion and technology is changing, the value of each item, and even the cost of each item, is in a constant state of flux.

Viewing a project as a large batch of work items makes it easy to apply return on investment, cost of delay and cost-benefit analysis at the item level rather than at the project level. The project delivers the first large batch of work, but requests keep on coming, some more valuable, some less. Just because the value was not seen before a particular 'sign-off' date does not make it worth less.

11.1 Value-seeking

Once individual items have their own value each becomes independent. Creation, delivery and, most importantly, post-delivery evaluation can occur even before work starts on other requests. This creates another feedback loop that can help to refine requests and inform decisions about what to do next.

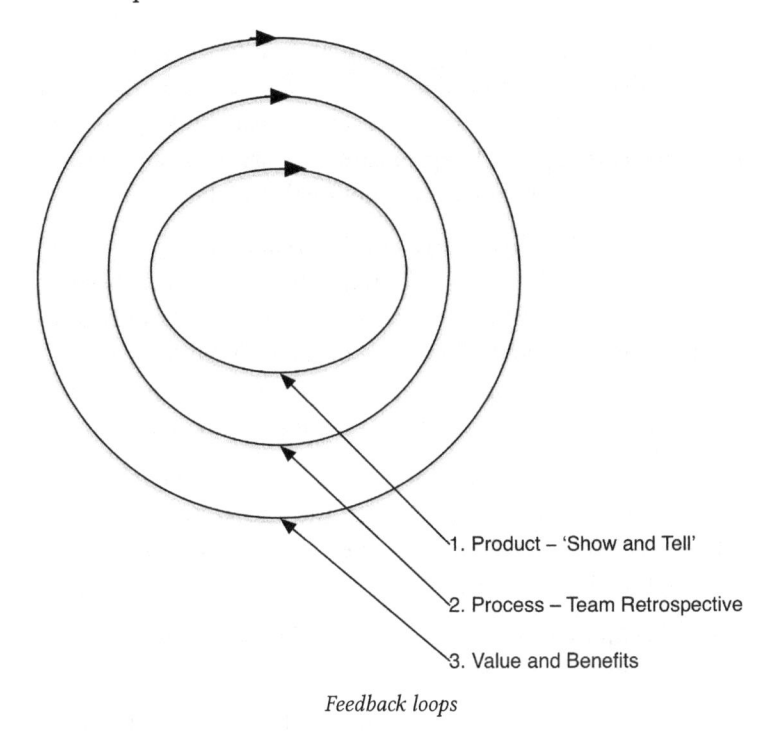

1. Product – 'Show and Tell'
2. Process – Team Retrospective
3. Value and Benefits

Feedback loops

Most agile teams will undertake regular 'show and tell' sessions to obtain feedback on what they have built. The better teams have a second feedback loop, a retrospective to improve their own way of working. Fewer teams implement a third feedback loop to ascertain the value and benefit they are delivering. A focus on the success troika renders this loop redundant, even dangerous.

Hopefully these feedback loops sound familiar. Sprints and Iterations – common to XP, Scrum and other agile methods – implement the same idea. So too does the Shewhart plan-do-check-act (PDCA) cycle, and the Lean Startup build-measure-learn loop. What is less obvious is that such feedback loops are incompatible with the idea of a project with a fixed amount of work, fixed dates and a fixed budget. Project thinking heavily discounts learning that happens after a 'start date', and disparages learning that endangers the notional 'end date'.

Requirements lists frequently contain requests left over from previous work and 'just in case' requests. When teams become value-seeking, looking at the benefit of work requests and checking the value delivered, then some of the original project work requests prove to be past their sell-by date. The acquisition of knowledge during the work causes requests to change again.

When teams become value-seeking the project model breaks down. There is no guarantee that the initial work requests will get delivered. Encouraging new ideas makes end dates meaningless. *Why end if you can still deliver competitive value?*

Failure becomes an important option. Why should a team continue working if it cannot deliver value?

A value-seeking team fails when it delivers less value than it costs to operate. When this happens the team may well reorientate itself and change its approach. A 'failure' is a message and an opportunity to change, to pivot. If the team cannot find value then it should wind itself down.

Contrast this with a team focused on the success troika. Such teams need not worry about whether their work delivers value. Schedule, cost and delivered items measure their success. Failure is a black mark that occurs when the schedule slips, costs overrun or deliveries don't measure up. The notion of 'failure' becomes subjective: tt is simply a label applied to stories that people tell to explain what happened.

For example, imagine a traditional team that starts to become value-seeking. The team starts a 'project' – a preselected batch of requirement requests that someone thinks valuable. After a few weeks they find there is no value in the work and decide to abort the project. Is this a success or failure?

On traditional success criteria it has failed. But from a value-delivery perspective the team has been successful, because of the costs not incurred in the pursuit of pointless work.

Today good agile teams often follow the value-seeking model within the confines of the project model and project language. One might argue that *if the team is doing the right thing, then what does it matter what words get used?*. But the existence of the project mindset outside of these teams – in the wider organization – hinders such a team. More importantly the project mindset, and language, creates dissonance and tensions between the different groups operating on different mental models.

This tension becomes most apparent when governance and portfolio review continue to use the project model. These criteria are inappropriate for judging the success or failure of an agile team.

11.2 Reducing risk

Disassembling and breaking projects down to their component pieces has another benefit. Not only does value increase, but risk is simultaneously reduced. An all-or-nothing, do-or-not-do endeavor inevitably pushes most risk to the end – *risk is tail-loaded.* Conversely, breaking a project down into multiple, beneficial increments pulls risk forward and spreads it more evenly over the duration of the work. Experience, skill and techniques like Walking Skeleton and MVP allow more risk to be front-loaded.

Imagine a project manager embarking on Project A. This has a value of $1,000,000 and analysis suggests there is a 30% risk of failure. Thus the weighted risk is $300,000.

Learning to spread value and risk over the entire work is a learned skill. Traditional project managers tend to push both towards the end of a project. But to keep this example simple let's assume value and risk are spread equally across the whole project.

Now suppose our PM splits the project into two: Project B worth $500,000 carries half the risk, 15%, and Project C carries the other half of the value and risk. Now the weighted risk is:

Project B: ($500,000 x 15%) = $75,000

Project C: ($500,000 x 15%) = = $75,000

Total = $75,000 + $75,000 = $150,000

Combined, Projects B and C carry half the risk of the original.

Next split the same work into five equal pieces, each of value $200,000 with 6% of the risk. Each piece now carries $12,000 of risk, so the total risk is $12,000 x 5 = $60,000. The greater the number of pieces the risk is spread over, the lower the total risk.

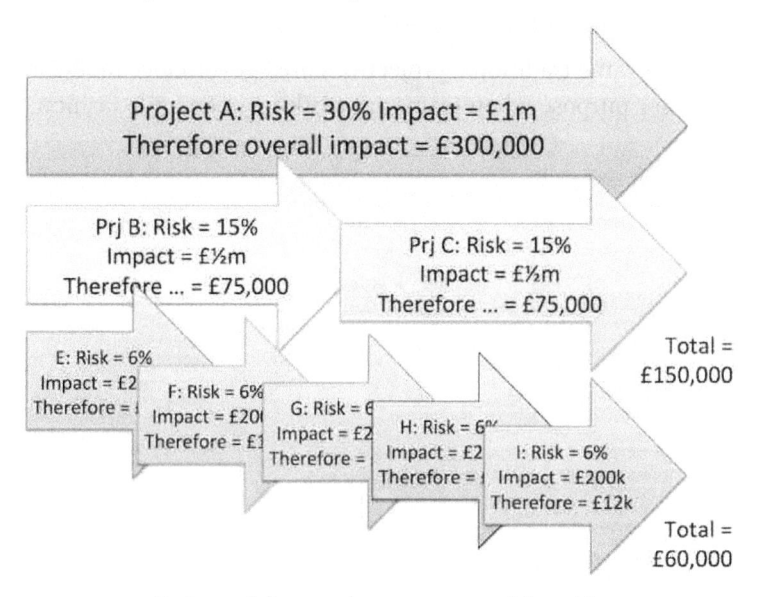

Project A: Risk = 30% Impact = £1m
Therefore overall impact = £300,000

Prj B: Risk = 15%
Impact = £½m
Therefore ... = £75,000

Prj C: Risk = 15%
Impact = £½m
Therefore ... = £75,000

Total = £150,000

E: Risk = 6%
Impact = £2
Therefore =

F: Risk = 6%
Impact = £20
Therefore = £1

G: Risk = 6
Impact = £2
Therefore =

H: Risk = 6%
Impact = £2
Therefore =

I: Risk = 6%
Impact = £200k
Therefore = £12k

Total = £60,000

Reduce risk by spreading it over more deliverables

Bundling more work into projects may look like a good thing, but it increases risk. Treating each individual work item as a 'mini-project' instead reduces risk.

Organizing as a series of mini-projects would carry overheads: project initiation, project shut-down, team formation, team dissolution and so on. So instead maybe the organization could organize an umbrella project within which there are mini-projects. Now how does one judge success?

While undoubtedly companies do organize agile teams as a series of mini-projects, they are not really using the project model. Nor are they addressing the criteria for success. By keeping the language and trappings of projects, but breaking the model, there is further confusion.

Ultimately, the traditional project-oriented governance model is not fit for purpose when teams are working in an agile fashion.

12. Debt thinking

Technical staff often use the term *technical debt* to describe situations in which the architecture, design or code is built in a substandard way. The way the term is commonly used implies that the person doing the work consciously cut corners in order to produce something more quickly: they 'borrowed' time from the future. In the future this time will need to be repaid and the design improved.

As an aside, it is worth pointing out that, while this is the way the term 'technical debt' gets used, it isn't what the originator, Ward Cunningham, meant by the term:

> 'There were plenty of cases where people would rush software out the door and learn things but never put that learning back into the program, and that by analogy was borrowing money thinking that you never had to pay it back'. Ward Cunningham[1]

Since software development is a continual learning exercise, Ward is pointing out that when one writes software one's own understanding improves. If one were to write the software again one would do it differently. If the software is to keep its core properties (flexibility, changeability and so on) then one owes it to the software to feed this new learning back to improve the software. The term for this is *refactoring*.

---

[1] http://wiki.c2.com/?WardExplainsDebtMetaphor

Given this understanding, it is inevitable that all software accumulates technical debt. But this is not how the term gets used colloquially. As used day-to-day, 'technical debt' implies conscious, deliberate, poor quality: borrowings from the future.

Unfortunately, this borrowing from the future is rarely repaid. Part of the reason why it is not repaid is the project model itself.

12.1 Debt is good

The project model does not consider the internal quality or state of the software product. The project criteria ignore, or even abuse, quality. Within the project model reducing internal quality – increasing common technical debt – is good, because it accelerates delivery schedules. The only side-effect is more moaning from technical staff.

After all, debt is not necessarily a bad thing; debt is often good, particularly in a business context. To many people in business – particularly bankers – debt is good. Debt allows you to grow business and improve earnings.

'Debt thinking' goes like this:

> "We are (time and money) poor, but we can borrow from tomorrow's riches. Rather than writing good code today we can save time (and money) by just getting something that works and later (when we are rich) we can come back and do all that good stuff we should do. (And by the way, if it turns out that our initiative fails, then we have saved effort and money.)"

This kind of debt thinking is similar to a mortgage:

> "I don't have the money to buy a house right now, but if I borrow the money from a bank I can pay back the money over time with the money I save on rent."

This thinking is ripe both among developers and those who employ developers. This leads to misunderstanding between engineers and non-engineers, and can even lead engineers into poor habits.

When an engineer says "This will add technical debt" the engineer thinks they are warning about something bad, but to a non-engineer (business person) debt is often the preferred form of funding. So buying new capability with (technical) debt sounds like a good deal.

Yet many engineers are the first to bemoan the fact that, despite the best intentions, they never get to pay back the debt. Instead they merely service the debt: that is to say, they (at best) repay the interest, but never the principle, so the debt remains. Indeed all too often the payments are not even sufficient to repay the interest, which gets added to the principle.

12.2 Why pay back debt?

With any debt the important question is *can you afford the payments?* The bigger the debt, the higher the interest rate, the greater the amount of today's resources (time, money, effort) needed to service the debt. Yesterday you borrowed so you could buy something beyond your resources, today you must devote some of your resources to pay those who provided the loan.

To many a business mind debt is not only natural: it is desirable. Generations of business leaders have been taught to embrace debt. Debt improves *earning per share* and increases profits.

Frequently companies never even plan to pay back financial debt. As long as cash-flow is sufficient to cover interest payments, then why do it? Surplus cash could pay for increased dividends to shareholders instead of repaying the bank, nNot to mention the preferential tax treatment most governments provide for debt.

Software engineers see debt as something to be repaid. But to the business mind debt is just another variable.

12.3 Payday loans

Debt thinking within a project is not free: it has significant costs. Debts incurred in building software are not like a mortgage. Mortgages typically have a low interest rate and are repaid steadily over a long period.

To a project manager technical debt is akin to an off-balance-sheet loan. There are no payments today: someone else, some other project, will need to deal with these debts at some unknown date in the future.

But 'debts' incurred within projects are not like mortgages or off-balance-sheet instruments that have little effect today. Project 'debts' are more like payday loans at exorbitant interest rates that need to be repaid soon. If they are not repaid soon, compound interest can quickly make the repayment schedule eye-watering.

Only those who are desperate (or financially naive) would accept a payday loan. Let me suggest those who willingly take on 'technical debt' are similarly desperate or technically naive. Very quickly – within the current project – the high interest rate can be crippling, while payments eat into the ability to do any useful work.

Time and time again software engineers relearn the lesson that higher quality is faster.

As Philip Crosby famously said, "Quality is free[2]". That is, doing a good 'quality' job will repay any extra effort. Even if quality isn't free, then as my friend Niels Malotaux likes to say, "Quality is cheaper [than the alternative]".

12.4 Technical liabilities

The time has come to retire the technical debt metaphor: in its place we should talk about *technical liabilities*. This is a small change in language with big implications.

Talking about 'technical debt' is loaded with problems. *When is a debt good? When is it bad? What is the interest rate? Do those who advocate incurring debt know what they are saying? And do you have a repayment plan?*

Simply changing our language from *technical debt* to *technical liability* removes these problems. Liability is something neither

---

[2] *Quality is Free: The Art of Making Quality Certain*, Crosby, 1980

business or technical folk consider good. If I look at my dictionary it tells me:

> Liability: 1. Subject to an obligation 2. Exposed to a possible risk 3. Responsible for ...and more...

Everyone can agree on these attributes, whether in a technical setting or a non-technical context.

Businesses have to list liabilities on their balance sheet, and reducing the liabilities produces a more attractive balance sheet. Debt, on the other hand, is listed as an asset on bank balance sheets. Even Apple sometimes chooses to issue debt rather than use capital.

Adopting the term 'technical liabilities' would allow 'technical debt' to return to Ward's original meaning.

Technical liabilities cost, because they create obligations, obligations that slow work down, obligations that must be repaid, and risks – one doesn't know when an obligation is going to disrupt work.

13. The quality problem

Defects are not free. Somebody makes them, and gets paid for making them. John Cage, composer, 1912-1992

The bottom line is that poor-quality software costs more to build and to maintain than high-quality software, and it can also degrade operational performance, increase user error rates, and reduce revenue by decreasing the ability handle customer transactions or attract additional clients'.

For the software industry, not only is quality free, as stated by Phil Crosby, but it benefits the entire economic situations of both developers and clients.* Jones, 2011[1].

Predicating thinking based on a faulty model has consequences. Perhaps the most damaging consequence of applying the project model to software development is the degradation of quality. It is doubtful if cutting quality helps to meet project deadlines, but it certainly creates costs for the future.

The idea that a project is a temporary undertaking is highly corrosive, because it leads to short-term thinking. Projects and

---

[1] *The Economics of Software Quality*, Jones, C., Bonsignour, B. and Subramanyam, J., 2011

those who manage them aim to meet a date and be 'done' one day. Hence any shortcut that reduces time is seen in a positive light. But such shortcuts frequently damage quality: bugs go unfixed, refactoring remains undone and technical debt piles up.

In the race to meet the deadline, thinking about what comes after the project gets discounted. Remaining issues and problems are left for the next 'project' and its teams to deal with. Any consideration given to these issues is seen as a luxury and gets dropped all too easily. (These issues are amplified when the project is undertaken by a subcontractor whose involvement will end with the project.)

Unfortunately making these cuts is damaging for the technical team building the product. As engineers many team members will feel good when they do a 'good job'; conversely, when asked to cut corners, they lose motivation. Once motivation goes a vicious circle begins and productivity falls. Project thinking leads to more quality reductions to get back on schedule, and work becomes more difficult as developers work around bugs and poor design. Consequently, motivation falls further and success becomes ever more distant.

A friend of mine visited a company where the project manager focused almost exclusively on the end date. She was constantly on the lookout for ways to shorten the schedule. But when it came to release time the same manager complained that the technical team didn't want to work late or put in extra effort to make the release happen.

Is it any surprise that if after months of requests to cut corners and endure compromises engineers shrug their shoulders at crunch times or when problems arise?

Quick definition of quality

My friend Tom Gilb would be quick to point out that software has many *qualities*. The term *non-functional requirements* is also used to describe the same attributes. The qualities vary from application to application. Speed of execution might be an important attribute for one app but not for another. Ease of use may be important for some but irrelevant to another.

I would argue though there are two attributes that all quality software exhibits:

- A limited number of defects: software with lots of bugs isn't really quality in my book.
- Maintainability: software that is not maintainable will not survive the test of time. Software that is difficult to maintain will be a fertile ground for bugs to breed. When bugs do occur, they will be hard to find and fix.

When I write about *software quality* I am specifically referring to these attributes. I do not doubt that software has many other qualities. I only say that these qualities are universally true for successful software.

13.1 Rethinking the quality tradeoff

Consider the common 'iron triangle' beloved by project managers:

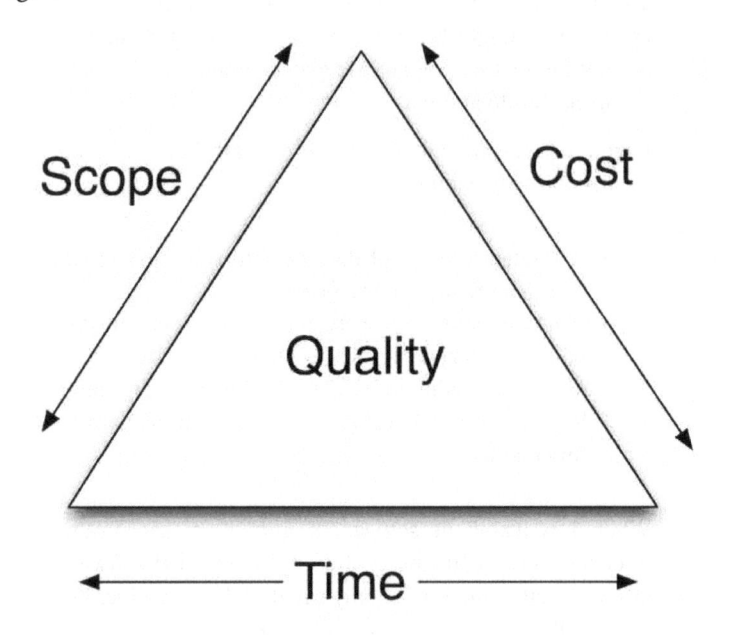

Classic project managers' iron triangle

While maybe not baked into the project model itself, there is a common maxim amongst project practitioners that:

Higher quality takes longer and costs more

They see a tradeoff: reducing quality reduces time (and perhaps budget). Unfortunately, in software, the maxim needs reversing:

Higher quality reduces total time and reduces costs

On any given day, for any given piece of functionality, doing a low-quality piece of work may indeed take less programmer time. If projects charged by the line of code delivered this way of working would make sense, but they do not.

Project myopia strikes again. A vicious circle starts: low-quality change quickly starts to increase time elsewhere: testers' time, developers' time, management time. In an attempt to make up lost time quality is cut further. All the time professional motivation is falling alongside quality.

People who try to accelerate development by deliberately cutting quality increase the time needed to do the work.

Projects with low defect potentials and high defect removal efficiency also have the shortest schedules, lowest costs and best customer satisfaction levels.
Jones, 2008[2]

Increasing quality accelerates development. Certainly it might take a little longer right now, but the pay-back comes quickly. This is simple really, even if it is counter-intuitive.

13.2 The cost of poor quality

Over time technical liabilities massively hinder the ability of organizations to change both the software and themselves. It

---
[2] *Applied Software Measurement*, Capers Jones, 2008

is worth a brief look at some of the ways liabilities make themselves felt.

In the short term, technical liabilities make it harder for programmers to do their job and modify existing code. Programming is a constant battle with complexity, and poor quality code increases complexity. Enhancements and changes become harder and therefore slower.

A poor-quality code base is a breeding ground for defects – bugs – simply because of complexity. Poor-quality code is not only more likely to be home to defects, but it is more difficult to fix when a defect is found.

Such code is harder to test because it tends to have more 'edge cases'. Because it is harder, the testing is slower. Testing slows and becomes harder to automate because poor-quality code tends to be more tightly coupled to other systems and subsystems. So it takes programmer time to create the defect in the first place, and tester time to find it and report it.

Then it gets really expensive. Managers need time to administer the defect – prioritize it, argue with other managers about priorities and severity, possibly schedule a fix, perhaps apologize to customers or report it up the organization. Defects may also place business-critical activities at risk, such as the launch of a new product.

Defects interrupt customers' work. Maybe they pay in lost time, maybe they pay directly in lost revenue, or in their own loss of credibility. Customers lose time when they report defects, and when customers log defects someone needs to record the defect – maybe the support desk, maybe a developer or a tester.

One defect may affect many customers. Many of those customers lose their time and money, and many customers will instigate many support calls as different customers report the same thing. Each report costs money and more money is spent identifying duplicates.

All the time a defect is sitting in a defect list somewhere it is costing money. Maybe it is costing customers again and again. At the very least it is taking managers time as they prioritize other defects ahead of it for a fix.

Finally, hopefully, the defect gets fixed. At which point it costs programmer time and tester time to validate that the fix is done, then time to notify stakeholders and make a release. It may also take customers time to switch over to the new version.

13.3 Who pays?

Introducing liabilities creates costs, and there is an ongoing cost-of-carry to liabilities. These costs grow over time and are recurring, but at any given time the cost of addressing the liability will be greater than the short-term costs.

When the liability is like a planned mortgage this seems reasonable: I cannot pay off the £250,000 I owe on my house today, so it is reasonable to repay a little of the balance and the interest, so that in 25 years I'll be done.

When the liability is like a payday loan and unpaid debt gets added to the principle, things get difficult. So the questions arises: *when will the debt be paid off, and by whom?*

Option #1 is for the current project to address the liability rather than treating it as off-balance-sheet. Given that the liability has already been incurred, fixing it might extend the current project schedule.

Option #2 is to leave the liability for a later project. This has the advantage that if the project never happens then the liability never needs addressing. But, as discussed earlier, successful software continues.

Leaving a liability open only makes sense if it is clear that the software is going to be unsuccessful. So working like this only makes sense if one believes that the final product will fail. This approach reeks of planning to fail.

Naturally, the latter project has the same conundrum as the first: continuing to carry the liability is probably less expensive than fixing it. Project myopia again: it is never attractive for a project to address existing problems, but it is attractive to leave them for a later project.

As the software is a long-term asset, perhaps even a platform on which the company is built, it is economically irrational to carry liabilities indefinitely.

Projects do not build to last. Success based on project management criteria may be at odds with the success of the business.

13.4 External costs

Technical debts, defect costs, costs of rework – these items are never logged against a project. There is no balance sheet that shows the value of the asset created and the outstanding liabilities. The cost of liabilities is invisible.

Overwhelmingly the cost of defects is what economists call *externalities*. Like a chemical plant that dumps polluted water into a public river and leaves the government to pay for the clean-up, the project model encourages software makers to let others carry the majority of costs associated with defects.

A better analogy may be an *off-balance-sheet liability*: defects that don't appear as liabilities on the creator's balance sheet. Instead, liabilities hide somewhere else. Someone else will need to pay to address the liability at a later, unspecified date.

One upside of the move towards software-as-a-service (SaaS) is that more of these costs are born by the software provider rather than the software user. A second benefit of SaaS is that because control stays with the provider, the provider has more control over fixing the defects.

13.5 There's no such thing as quick and dirty

It should be clear by now that there is no such thing as *quick and dirty* software changes. There are only *dirty and slow*.

What might look like a quick fix is more likely to resemble a payday loan that will very quickly start eating up capacity and making subsequent work more expensive. At best such changes shift the cost from the creators to the customers and users. Pushing the work off the balance sheet creates risks.

Unfortunately, the project model encourages off-balance-sheet liabilities and risks, and as commonly practiced, encourages payday loans.

14. Programmes not projects

One of the comments that is often made when I present the #NoProjects ideas is "Isn't that just programme management?" Indeed, in a few organizations, many of the ideas contained within here are realized in the form of *programmes*. However, this is far from universal.

In many organizations 'programme management' is a form of 'very large project management'. In fact, the term 'programme' – plus the associated 'programme manager' and 'programme management office' (PMO) are all somewhat elastic terms meaning different things in different organizations. It is worth for a moment considering these terms.

Note: It is useful here to use the English-English spelling of 'programme' – as opposed to the American-English 'program' – to distinguish it from a computer 'program' (that is, an application or process), which is spelled 'program' in all dialects of English. Both because I am English and because I find it useful to differentiate between a 'computer program' and a 'management programme', I will stick with the English-English spellings.

14.1 What does a Programme Manager do?

In some organizations the title *Programme Manager* is used to denote a Senior Project Manager. The role is the same as a Project Manager, but being more senior the Programme Manager is entrusted with larger and more costly projects.

In other organizations a Programme Manager is the manager of a 'programme of work', which is itself constructed from multiple projects. In these cases the Programme Manager directs multiple projects, each of which probably has its own Project Manager.

In all these cases the programme is a super-sized project, and as such is expected to end eventually. Like a project, these kinds of programme have a nominal end date.

However, I was taught in college that a *programme*, although akin to a project, is *not* expected to end. I think of the US Visa Waiver Programme that allows Europeans such as myself to travel to the USA without a formal visa. This programme has existed since 1986, and while Congress could terminate the programme it seems likely to remain in existence for the foreseeable future.

14.2 The Programme Management Office

The abbreviation PMO may refer to a project management office or a programme management office. I consider the two terms to be synonymous, because very few organizations seem to draw a hard distinction between them. In my experience the two terms are interchangeable. I am sure there are organizations within which the difference is important, but I have never experienced one. Anyway, the confusion over the PMO name is just the start: let's move on.

Although the expression PMO can conjure up visions of a war-room decorated in Gantt charts and populated by serious people in serious clothes tracking the action, like one of those World War II control rooms tracking convoys or bomber attacks, the reality is very different.

At one extreme the PMO may be little more than admin support, a place where pens and paperclips are stored, perhaps populated by one or two people who would once have been called secretaries or clerks. Once a week they become busy as all the project reports arrive, are sorted and dispatched again.

The other extreme isn't the Battle-of-Britain war-room: it's more likely to contain a few experienced project managers who support projects with expert advice. They may still collect the weekly reports, but they may package them into a unified report.

High-powered PMOs may also fulfill a governance and/or portfolio function, collating weekly project reports and reviewing them. Low-powered PMOs may also gather weekly reports, but probably just put them in a single binder or PowerPoint presentation for more senior managers.

Somewhere in the middle is probably *your* PMO.

> **PMO makes it look good**
>
> A few years ago some PMO staff attended an agile introduction session I was running. At one point I made my usual comment that "Agile working makes it harder to hide problems" when discussing project status reports. To my horror one of the Programme Managers replied:
>
> "But it is our job to make the project reports look good."
>
> He wasn't joking either. This particular PMO had come to see its role as sugar-coating bad news.

14.3 So what is a programme?

As you might be expecting by now, *programme* is a rather ill-defined term in practice. Because it is ill-defined, it is hard to reason about programme management in general.

But there *is* a discipline called Programme Management. Within that discipline, there are a lot of good ideas. Some overlap with projects, some with portfolio management, some with governance and some with #NoProjects.

So programme management is no silver bullet, and those who say "#NoProjects is nothing new – it's programme management" have a point. But since the practice and implementation of programme management is so variable, something else is needed – at least until such time as programme management becomes more consistent.

15. Personal changes

> *Do not think of today's failures, but of the success that may come tomorrow. You have set yourselves a difficult task, but you will succeed if you persevere, and you will find a joy in overcoming obstacles – a delight in climbing rugged paths, which you would perhaps never know if you did not sometimes slip backward – if the road was always smooth and pleasant.* Helen Keller, author and activist, 1880-1968

There are a few things you can do right now to start implementing the ideas described in this book. The first two of these you as an individual can achieve entirely through your own words and actions.

The third may be directly within your power if you have sufficient authority. If you do not, you can at least start asking relevant questions and encouraging those with the power to open up what they already know or help them to come to a common understanding.

The fourth is very dependent on your position. You may be able to do this immediately, or you may need to work towards helping others take action.

15.1 Stop saying "project"

Simply ridding yourself of the language of projects is a good start. The word itself causes confusion, because it brings assumptions and models into play that are not applicable. So stop using the vocabulary of projects.

Where the vocabulary cannot be removed the different parties need to agree on what is meant by the term 'project'. It may help to invent new language to describe what the team does. In defining what a 'project' is, it helps to agree shared success criteria, rather than having each individual make their own assumptions.

15.2 Collections of small things

Work to do. Lots of little bits of work to do.

Stop seeing 'projects' as large all-or-nothing endeavors: instead see them as a collection of lots of little things.

If this seems difficult, then good, you are making a start. Just start by trying to break things up. You might want to learn more about methods for doing this. Perhaps find yourself a mentor, or go on a training course; at the very least read a book, perhaps my own *Little Book of Requirements and User Stories*.

15.3 Public success criteria

Be sure the objectives and success criteria are clear for any work your team is undertaking. Go further: make sure these are very public – post the objectives on a wall where everyone can see them!

When goals are intangible teams need to find ways to make them tangible. Conversations about benefit and value need to continue throughout the work because the goal itself is hard to pin down.

15.4 Value estimates

Each of the *small pieces of work to do* should have a statement or estimate of value. Estimates are good enough here; they can drive prioritization. Once you have placed a value on a work item, consider how its value may change over time. If you do it sooner, does it add value? How does value change when work gets delayed?

When value estimates are in place you can start to evaluate the post-delivery results. Doing so creates an additional feedback loop. Use the results of this feedback to calibrate future value estimates. (My *Little Book of Requirements and User Stories* discusses time-value profiles and value estimates in more detail.)

15.5 More than agile

These suggestions might not come as a surprise to those versed in agile: they parallel advice that has circulated for years. Here however I am applying the advice at the next level up: iterations are not just for coders – they should be applied at the management level too.

For many organizations 'agile' is something that happens within a project box. The organization plans projects and projects get delivered. Whether what happens within the box is 'agile' or something else is of little concern to the project-planning process.

Rather than thinking of 'agile projects' and doing all the good 'agile stuff' within the confines of a project, *I am suggesting that the organization changes how it understands work altogether.*

15.6 Stronger together

Some of these suggestions lock together. For example, if you keep your teams together it is easier to do lots of little things. If you break your teams up after every little job you will never have productive teams and management will spend all their time scheduling people. Instead, have standing teams and bring the work to the teams.

The build/destroy approach overvalues 'economies of scale' and fails to take advantage of the lower-risk, faster-delivery approach that agile proposes.

Some of these changes can be done immediately: there are things you can start doing right now by yourself. Going further means changing not just your own mental model, but the mental models of those around you. As the Keynes' quote with which I opened this book says, practical men need to free themselves of outdated ideas.

Given that project thinking has dominated the approach of technology management for the last 30 years, moving away from projects is going to require some changes in management thinking.

15.7 Continuous Digital

For those who want to learn more about organizing and managing in a project-free environment, I recommend my other book, *Continuous Digital*.

Continuous Digital describes a management model for managing work and organizations without using projects. Once upon a time it was a continuation of this book. *Continuous Digital*[1] stands alone, but it also starts where this book finishes – right here.

---

[1] https://leanpub.com/cdigital/

Continuous Digital

Continue the #NoProjects story with Continuous Digital continues

Allan Kelly's latest book:

- Why digital business need a new model of software development
- A full description of the Continuous model

Ebook draft available on LeanPub[2] and pre-order on Amazon[3].

---
[2] https://leanpub.com/cdigital/
[3] https://www.amazon.co.uk/Allan-Kelly/e/B001JSFJEE

Evolution of a meme

> *What is #Noprojects? The alignment of activities to outcomes measured by value, constrained by guiding principles and supported by continuous delivery technologies.* Evan Leybourn, 2017

This book and the #NoProjects name itself have been evolving from day one. In fact, the evolution of #NoProjects is a case study in the coevolution of problem and solution.

No Projects started as a critique of project thinking, but was criticized for not offering solutions. It didn't, but then not every problem has a solution, or at least not yet.

In crafting a coherent answer to this critique my thinking – and the thinking of Evan Leybourn, Josh Arnold and Steve Smith – advanced.

For me, #NoProjects gave way to *Stream-Based Development*, then *Beyond Projects*, Josh evolved towards #ProjectLess, while Evan has stayed with the *No Projects* moniker even as his thinking has advanced.

The more I looked at #NoProjects, the solution and the problem, the more I saw that it was intimately linked with Marc Andreessen's 'Software is eating the world' hypothesis. A hypothesis that is now embedded in one word: *Digital*. Or perhaps two: *digital business*.

For me, #NoProjects evolved into *Continuous Digital* – the child of agile and Digital.

Many of the chapters in this book predate *Continuous Digital* and formed the initial draft of that book. As *Continuous Digital* grew into its own book it became clear that *Project Myopia* was its own critique and deserved its own book.

Continuous Digital solves multiple problems. The problem of what to do instead of projects. The problem of extending agile and Continuous Delivery.

And most of all: the problem of how to organize a business that lives and dies by its ability to deliver digital products.

This book is a critique. If you are looking for solutions, please buy Continuous Digital[4].

---

[4] https://leanpub.com/cdigital/

About the author

Allan inspires digital teams to effectively deliver better products through Agile technologies. These approaches shorten lead times, improve predictability, increase value, improve quality and reduce risk. He believes that improving development requires broad view of interconnected activities. Most of his work is with innovative teams, smaller companies - including scale-ups; he specialises in product development and engineering. He uses a mix of experiential training and ongoing consulting.

He is the originator of Retrospective Dialogue Sheets[5], the author of several books including: "Xanpan - team centric Agile Software Development" and "Business Patterns for Software Developers", and a regular conference speaker.

Contact: allan@allankelly.net

Twitter: @allankellynet[6]

Web: http://www.allankelly.net/[7]

Blog: http://blog.allankellynet/[8]

---

[5] http://www.dialoguesheets.com/
[6] https://twitter.com/allankellynet
[7] http://www.allankelly.net/
[8] http://blog.allankellynet/

Also by Allan Kelly

Little Book of Requirements and User Stories

Available from your local Amazon[9]

Xanpan: Team Centric Agile Software Development

Ebook: https://leanpub.com/xanpan[10]

Print on demand: Lulu.com[11]

And your local Amazon[12]

Business Patterns for Software Developers

Published by John Wiley & Sons

Available in all good bookshops and at Amazon[13]

---

[9] https://www.amazon.com/Little-Book-about-Requirements-Stories-ebook/dp/B06XZZ6BQD

[10] https://leanpub.com/xanpan

[11] http://www.lulu.com/shop/allan-kelly/xanpan-team-centric-agile-software-development/paperback/product-22271338.html

[12] https://www.amazon.com/s/ref=nb_sb_noss?url=search-alias%3Daps&field-keywords=Xanpan

[13] https://www.amazon.com/Business-Patterns-Software-Developers-Allan-ebook/dp/B007U2ZT7K

Changing Software Development: Learning to Be Agile

Available in all good bookshops and at Amazon[14]

[14] https://www.amazon.com/Changing-Software-Development-Learning-Become/dp/047051504X

Acknowledgements

Thanks to the programme committee of the 2013 Project and Analysis 'PAM Summit' conference in Krakow, Poland, whose request for a talk to business analysts and project managers challenged me to think long and hard about project managers, and therefore projects. Thank you to the BCS PROMS-G (Project Management Special Interest Group), who asked me to speak to their members. It was in creating these presentations that the nucleus of #NoProjects was formed.

Many thanks to 'agile' Steve Smith and Joshua Arnold here in London for an ongoing Twitter dialogue that became the #NoProjects hypothesis. My original thinking focused on projects as a redundant management model; Steve and Josh put more emphasis on risk management and cost of delay. The three threads fused into one and I can no longer tell which of us added which ideas, or who first used the #NoProjects hashtag. Thanks too to Evan Leybourn, who at about the same time was having the same thoughts on the other side of the planet.

In late 2015 Vasco Duarte asked me to write something about #NoProjects for the #NoEstimates newsletter. Till then I'd written relatively little about #NoProjects. The term started to appear in blog postings sometime in 2013, but most of the thinking had appeared in conference presentations. What started as a short essay eventually topped 23 A4 pages. Most of that article is contained in this book, although it has been updated and refactored in places.

A word of caution: #NoProjects is not #NoEstimates. There is a strong synergy between the two but they are different ideas and have different solutions. Still, thanks must go to the fathers of #NoEstimates, Duarte Vasco and Woody Zuill, who spotted the synergies and adopted #NoProjects. Special thanks to Duarte for asking me to write about #NoProjects for the #NoEstimates community.

Several other people have encouraged me along the path towards this book and deserve to be mentioned: Kevlin Henney and Sunish Chabba spring to mind. Thanks too to Andy Longshaw, John Clapham and Matthew Skelton, who shared the implementation of stream teams on an undertaking that will remain nameless.

As noted in the book my thinking on governance has been strongly influenced by Chris Matts. Through conversations and his blog posts Chris has provided many of the missing pieces, both on governance and more broadly.

Some of the early readers have sent me feedback too: thanks to Gwendal Tanguy, Dmitry Ledentsov, Klaus Marquardt and others.

Nearly there... Thanks to the folk at LeanPub for the technology that makes this book possible and which demonstrates the ideas of #NoProjects so well. Beyond LeanPub I am grateful to Steve Rickaby of WordMongers for copyediting and Anton Fimaier for the cover illustration.

And like all authors, thanks to the family – Tasya, Grisha and Anton – for allowing Daddy to indulge himself.